plurall

Parabéns!
Agora você faz parte do **Plurall**, a plataforma digital do seu livro didático! No **Plurall**, você tem acesso gratuito aos recursos digitais deste livro por meio do seu computador, celular ou *tablet*. Além disso, você pode contar com a nossa tutoria *on-line* sempre que surgir alguma dúvida sobre as atividades e os conteúdos deste livro.

Incrível, não é mesmo?
Venha para o **Plurall** e descubra uma nova forma de estudar!
Baixe o aplicativo do **Plurall** para Android e IOS ou acesse www.plurall.net e cadastre-se utilizando o seu código de acesso exclusivo:

AAAG2ZYGY

Este é o seu código de acesso Plurall. Cadastre-se e ative-o para ter acesso aos conteúdos relacionados a esta obra.

@plurallnet
@plurallnetoficial

SOMOS EDUCAÇÃO

Hello! teens

STAGE 7

ELIETE CANESI MORINO

Graduada pela Pontifícia Universidade Católica de São Paulo em Língua e Literatura Inglesas e Tradução e Interpretação.

Especialização em Língua Inglesa pela International Bell School of London.

Pós-graduada em Metodologia da Língua Inglesa pela Faculdade de Tecnologia e Ciência.

Atuou como professora da rede particular de ensino e em projetos comunitários.

RITA BRUGIN DE FARIA

Graduada pela Faculdade de Arte Santa Marcelina e pela Faculdade Paulista de Artes.

Especialização em Língua Inglesa pela International Bell School of London.

Pós-graduada em Metodologia da Língua Inglesa pela Faculdade de Tecnologia e Ciência.

Especialista em alfabetização, atuou como professora e coordenadora pedagógica das redes pública e particular de ensino.

editora ática

editora ática

Direção Presidência: Mario Ghio Júnior
Direção de Conteúdo e Operações: Wilson Troque
Direção editorial: Luiz Tonolli e Lidiane Vivaldini Olo
Gestão de projeto editorial: Mirian Senra
Gestão de área: Alice Silvestre
Coordenação: Renato Malkov
Edição: Ana Lucia Militello, Carla Fernanda Nascimento (assist.), Caroline Santos, Danuza Dias Gonçalves, Maiza Prande Bernardello, Milena Rocha (assist.), Sabrina Cairo Bileski
Planejamento e controle de produção: Patrícia Eiras e Adjane Queiroz
Revisão: Hélia de Jesus Gonsaga (ger.), Kátia Scaff Marques (coord.), Rosângela Muricy (coord.), Ana Curci, Ana Paula C. Malfa, Arali Gomes, Brenda T. M. Morais, Diego Carbone, Gabriela M. Andrade, Luís M. Boa Nova, Patricia Cordeiro; Amanda T. Silva e Bárbara de M. Genereze (estagiárias)
Arte: Daniela Amaral (ger.), Catherine Saori Ishihara (coord.) e Letícia Lavôr (edit. arte)
Diagramação: Estúdio Lima
Iconografia e tratamento de imagem: Sílvio Kligin (ger.), Claudia Bertolazzi (coord.), Evelyn Torrecilla (pesquisa iconográfica), Cesar Wolf e Fernanda Crevin (tratamento)
Licenciamento de conteúdos de terceiros: Thiago Fontana (coord.), Flavia Zambon e Angra Marques (licenciamento de textos), Erika Ramires, Luciana Pedrosa Bierbauer, Luciana Cardoso Sousa e Claudia Rodrigues (analistas adm.)
Ilustrações: Fido Nesti, Filipe Rocha, Henrique Heráclio, Nik Neves e Ricardo J. Souza
Cartografia: Eric Fuzii (coord.), Robson Rosendo da Rocha (edit. arte)
Design: Gláucia Koller (ger.), Talita Guedes (proj. gráfico e capa) e Gustavo Vanini (assist. arte)
Foto de capa: Vasily Pindyurin/Getty Images

Todos os direitos reservados por Editora Ática S.A.
Avenida das Nações Unidas, 7221, 3º andar, Setor A
Pinheiros – São Paulo – SP – CEP 05425-902
Tel.: 4003-3061
www.atica.com.br / editora@atica.com.br

Dados Internacionais de Catalogação na Publicação (CIP)

```
Morino, Eliete Canesi
   Hello teens 7º ano / Eliete Canesi Morino, Rita Brugin
de Faria. - 8. ed. - São Paulo : Ática, 2019.

   Suplementado pelo manual do professor.
   Bibliografia.
   ISBN: 978-85-08-19334-9 (aluno)
   ISBN: 978-85-08-19335-6 (professor)


   1.   Língua inglesa (Ensino fundamental). I. Faria,
Rita Brugin de. II. Título.

2019-0113                                 CDD: 372.652
```

Julia do Nascimento - Bibliotecária - CRB-8/010142

2020
Código da obra CL 742203
CAE 648311 (AL) / 648310 (PR)
8ª edição
3ª impressão
De acordo com a BNCC.

Impressão e acabamento EGB Editora Gráfica Bernardi Ltda

Uma publicação

WELCOME, STUDENTS, TO HELLO! TEENS 7

Hello!

A língua inglesa está cada vez mais presente no nosso dia a dia. Ela chega até nós por intermédio dos mais diversos canais de comunicação e, assim, a todo momento estamos ouvindo, lendo e falando espontaneamente em inglês.

Em virtude da evolução da tecnologia, as distâncias tornaram-se virtuais e o inglês é o idioma mais utilizado por pessoas de diferentes nacionalidades que querem se comunicar entre si.

A **Coleção Hello! Teens**, escrita para você, um adolescente do mundo contemporâneo, quer motivá-lo a aprender inglês por meio de temas instigantes associados a atividades que facilitarão sua aprendizagem.

Participe ativamente das aulas refletindo e interagindo com seus colegas e desfrute de todos os benefícios que esta aprendizagem pode lhe proporcionar!

As autoras

CONTENTS

	WORD WORK	FOCUS ON LANGUAGE	LISTEN AND SPEAK	READ AND WRITE	TIPS FOR LIFE
WELCOME! P. 6	Content review from Hello! Teens 6				
UNIT 1 Studying Abroad P. 10	Benefits of studying abroad and school subjects	Present Continuous (all forms), -ing verbs (general rules), possessive adjectives	Testimonials of exchange students / Personal introduction	Exchange student application form / Create a library application form	Be a nice person
UNIT 2 The Sustainable Generation P. 24	Clothes and shoes	Review Simple Present (all forms), demonstrative pronouns (this, that, these, those), How much...? (prices)	Donation project organized by students / Create a donation project	Donation blog post / Write a blog post inviting people for a bazaar	Donate!
REVIEW	Units 1 and 2 - p. 38 and 39				
UNIT 3 Can I Have the Menu, Please? P. 40	Meals, food and beverages	Review Simple Present verb to be (all forms), subject and object pronouns, would like... (all forms)	Ordering food on-line / Create dialog to order food on-line	One-day restaurant menu / Create a healthy menu	Making the right choice
UNIT 4 Enjoying Art P. 54	Different kinds of art expressions	Modal verbs: can (present) and could (past), Wh- questions (why, what, where, who)	Fans talking about their idols abilities / Talk about things you can/can't do	Street art Eduardo Kobra's mural / Write a description of a classmate's work of art	Talents and skills
REVIEW	Units 3 and 4 - p. 68 and 69				

	WORD WORK	FOCUS ON LANGUAGE	LISTEN AND SPEAK	READ AND WRITE	TIPS FOR LIFE
UNIT 5 Weather Conditions P. 70	Weather conditions, seasons of the year	Verb to be – Simple Past (all forms), Simple Past expressions, prepositions of time (in, on, at)	Weather forecast for the weekend; Share information about your last trip	Newspaper weather headlines; Write a newspaper headline	Climate change
UNIT 6 It Was an Amazing Party! P. 84	Party items and present ideas	Simple Past – Regular verbs (all forms), -ed rules, short answers, some, any, How much...?, How many...?	Easy cupcake recipe; Create a dialog using past tense and expressions	Chocolate cake recipe; Write a special family recipe	Being a conscious consumer
REVIEW		Units 5 and 6 - p. 98 and 99			
UNIT 7 Did You Know...? P. 100	Great inventions	Simple Past – irregular verbs (all forms)	Great inventors and their inventions; Create a timeline	Marie Curie biography; Write a biography of an inventor	Necessity and inventions
UNIT 8 What Time Was Sayuri's Flight? P. 114	Traveling and airport related vocabulary	Past Continuous x Simple Past, when and while, telling the time, linking words (and, but, because, when, then)	Airport check-in and safety instructions; Emergency procedures discussion	Travel blog post; Write a post about your trip	Respect diversity!
REVIEW		Units 7 and 8 - p. 128 and 129			

EXTRA PRACTICE P. 130
PROJECTS P. 138
FUN ACTIVITIES P. 142
IRREGULAR VERBS P. 150
GLOSSARY P. 146
GRAMMAR HELPER P. 151
WORKBOOK P. 161

1. Look at the Browns' family tree. Then complete the sentences.

a. _____ are Kitty's brothers. They love to play sports and video game.

b. John is Kitty's _____. He loves to cook for his family.

c. Liz is Kitty's _____. She loves her family and she works from home.

d. Mary is Kitty's _____. She is very energetic and she loves jogging in the park.

e. Paul is Kitty's _____. He loves reading mystery novels.

f. _____ are Kitty's paternal grandparents. They seem like cool grandparents.

LANGUAGE TIPS

> Two other words used to say "father" in English are **daddy** and **dad**. Also, instead of "mother", we can use: **mom**, **mommy**, **mum** (British English), or **mam** (spoken in Ireland and some regions in England). Those words are spelled differently but are pronounced almost the same way.

2. Now draw your family tree and present it to your classmates.

3 Look at the picture and write the names of the rooms and the furnishings. Then listen and repeat the words.

bathroom   sink   living room   stove   dining room
air conditioning   bed   table   kitchen   fridge   bedroom   bathtub
office room   desk   sofa   chair

Rooms in a house	Furnishings
a.	a.
b.	b.
c.	c.
d.	d.
e.	e.
f.	f.
	g.
	h.
	i.
	j.

4 Listen and circle the numbers.

a. 88   98
b. 17   70
c. 155   365
d. 1 500 1 050
e. 3 000 300

SEVEN 7

5 In pairs, write the words in the correct column.

> horseback riding   gray   thank you   please   purple
> eighty-eight   hello   third   fifth   park
> stadium   starfish   table tennis   grandma   good morning
> alligator   basketball   canoeing   highlighter   grapes
> corn   mechanical pencil   one hundred   father

School objects	Sports	Colors	Around town
_____	_____	_____	_____
_____	_____	_____	_____

Camping activities	Food	Polite words	Animal world
_____	_____	_____	_____
_____	_____	_____	_____

Greetings	Ordinal numbers	Cardinal numbers	Family members
_____	_____	_____	_____
_____	_____	_____	_____

6 Complete Magda's daily routine using the words from the box. Then listen and check.

> have   starts   bed   go   dressed   shower   lunch   play
> classmates   Jamaica   do   watch   get up   dinner

My name is Magda. I'm from Kingston, in _____. This is a typical day in my life:

I _____ at 7:00 a.m., get _____ for school and _____ breakfast. My school _____ at eight thirty. I have _____ at 1:00 p.m. In the afternoon, I _____ soccer with my _____ at school. Then I _____ home at 4:00 p.m. When I get home, I take a _____ and I _____ my homework. I have _____ at seven p.m. Then I _____ TV and go to _____ at 10:00 p.m.

7 Look at the picture and answer. What are they doing?

| sing | dance | eat | drink | talk | play |

a. Jason and Carol _____ about school.

b. Jim _____ a hip-hop song.

c. Allan and Jodie _____ happily.

d. Leo and Daniel _____ soda.

e. Lucy _____ the electric guitar.

f. Sayuri and Mia _____ sandwiches.

8 Read and underline the correct form of the verbs.
a. Maria doesn't **get up/gets up** at 6:40 a.m.
b. She **play/plays** the guitar.
c. Tom and Teddy **live/lives** in a small house.
d. Leo **don't/doesn't** play the drums.
e. **Do/Does** the English class start at 8 o'clock?
f. Liza **live/lives** in a large apartment.

Let's play **Sausage Game**.

Unit 1 STUDYING ABROAD

1. Look at the picture and talk to your classmates.

   a. What does "study abroad" mean to you?

   b. Can you think of five reasons for studying abroad?

   c. Do you want to study abroad in the future? In which country?

2. Read and listen to the dialog. Then act out.

Kitty: Hi, everybody! I have a big surprise for you.

Sayuri: Hello!

Kitty: This is my e-pal Sayuri. She is here as an exchange student now. She is our new classmate!

Everybody: Hello, Sayuri!

Teacher: Sayuri, come and introduce yourself to your classmates, please.

Sayuri: My name is Sayuri Aisawa. I'm from Tokyo, Japan, but now I'm living in New York. It's nice to meet all of you.

Everybody: Nice to meet you, too, Sayuri!

Sayuri: *Arigato*… Oh! I mean, thank you!

Carol: What are you doing in the U.S.?

Sayuri: I'm here to learn about the American culture and way of life. And to improve my English, of course. Also, I want to make new friends!

Mark: What is your favorite school subject?

Sayuri: It's Art. I'm good at making *origami* and *ikebana*. I also teach elderly people how to make *origami* at an NGO.

Steve: And what is your favorite sport, Sayuri?

Sayuri: My favorite sport is baseball. Baseball is a popular sport in Japan.

Teacher: It's important to learn the differences between cultures, and to respect them.

Everybody: Welcome to Dalton High School.

Sayuri: Thank you!

3. Check the correct alternatives to complete the sentence.

Sayuri is studying abroad to…

- ○ learn a new culture.
- ○ teach *origami*.
- ○ improve her English.
- ○ make new friends.

THINKING AHEAD

1 Look at the map below. What is its main objective?

○ To show the importance of some languages.

○ To show the level of proficiency in English by country.

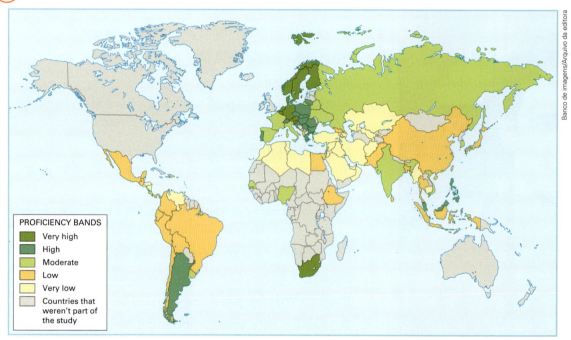

Available at: <www.ef.com/__/~/media/centralefcom/epi/downloads/full-reports/v8/ef-epi-2018-english.pdf>. Accessed on: Feb. 7, 2019.

2 Match the sentences according to the information on the map.

a. In Sweden,   ○ the proficiency in English is very low.

b. In Brazil,   ○ the proficiency in English is moderate.

c. In Malaysia,   ○ the proficiency in English is low.

d. In Venezuela,   ○ the proficiency in English is high.

e. In Nigeria,   ○ the proficiency in English is very high.

3 Based on the map, check the wrong statements.

a. ○ In South America, only Argentina has a high proficiency in English.

b. ○ In Asia, most of the countries have a very high proficiency in English.

c. ○ In Europe, there isn't a country where the proficiency in English is low.

d. ○ In Africa, there is no country where the proficiency in English is very high.

4 Why is it important for a country to have a good level of proficiency in English? In pairs, list three reasons and share them with your classmates.

A WORD WORK

1. Listen and match the benefits of studying abroad to the pictures.

immerse in a new language   eat typical food   make new friends at school
visit touristic attractions   expand your world view   learn about a new culture and its people
experience different styles of learning   watch interesting celebrations

a.

b.

c.

d.

e.

f.

g.

h.

2 Match the school subjects to the sentences.

a. Computer Science
b. English
c. Physical Education (P.E.)
d. Mathematic (Math)
e. Geography
f. History
g. Science
h. Art
i. Music

- ( ) Three times twenty is equal to sixty.
- ( ) Click here to download the program.
- ( ) Brazil is in the Southern Hemisphere.
- ( ) The French Revolution began in 1789.
- ( ) **I**, **you**, **he**, **she**, **it**, **we** and **they** are pronouns.
- ( ) Keeping fit is important for a healthy body and mind.
- ( ) Beethoven composed only one opera, called *Fidelio*.
- ( ) *Mona Lisa* is one of Leonardo da Vinci's famous paintings.
- ( ) This substance is composed of one type of atom and molecule.

TIME FOR A GAME

Let's play **Bingo** and **Brainstorm**!

FOCUS ON LANGUAGE

1 Read the comic strip below and check the correct statement.

a. ◯ Jon is a stand-up comedian.
b. ◯ Garfield wants to run with Jon.
c. ◯ Garfield is describing Jon's actions.

2 Pay attention to Garfield's statements. What do they have in common?

a. ◯ They describe actions that happened in the past.
b. ◯ They describe actions happening at the time of speaking.

3 Look at the chart below and do the following activity.

Present Continuous		
Affirmative		
I	am	studying abroad.
Interrogative		
Am	I	studying abroad?
Negative		
I	am not	studying abroad.
-ing verbs (General Rules)		

1. **study** – She is study**ing** abroad.
2. **practice** – The team is not practic**ing** for the big game.
3. **stop** – He is stop**ping** at the corner.
4. **enter** – Is the teacher enter**ing** the room?

Go to page 151.

In the comic strip above, the sentence "Now he's singing" is in the _____ of the Present Continuous.

a. ◯ negative form   b. ◯ affirmative form   c. ◯ interrogative form

FIFTEEN 15

4 Look at the scene. Then read the text and circle the correct words or expressions.

Today is a regular day in Saint Patrick School. Lucy and Ann **is/are** working together in their project. Mary **is writing/wrote** a composition. John **is/isn't** taking a Math test. **Louis is wearing/Is Louis wearing** his favorite green T-shirt.

5 What are these people doing? Write sentences using the expressions from the box.

> do homework   play baseball   read a magazine
> swim   study Science   eat a sandwich

a.

_____
_____

b.

_____
_____

c.

_____
_____

d.

_____
_____

e.

_____
_____

f.

_____
_____

6 Match the questions to the answers.

Joana is filling up a form to apply for the Summer School Games.

a. How old are you?
b. What is your full name?
c. What is your favorite school subject?
d. Where are you from?
e. Where is your hometown?
f. When is your birthday?

◯ I'm twelve years old.
◯ My birthday is on September 5th.
◯ I'm from Brazil, South America.
◯ My favorite school subject is P.E.
◯ My hometown is in Rio de Janeiro.
◯ My full name is Joana Cardoso.

7 Write questions according to the answers.

a. **A.** _____
   B. Her favorite sport is running.

b. **A.** _____
   B. My Math test is tomorrow.

c. **A.** _____
   B. Yes, he is making new friends at school.

d. **A.** _____
   B. No, I'm not playing basketball. I'm playing volleyball.

e. **A.** _____
   B. My favorite school subject is Art.

f. **A.** _____
   B. He is eleven years old.

8. Look at the pictures and check.

Benjamin is carrying some History books to **his** best friend, Hilton.

Daisy is telling **her** aunt Sally the good news about school.

The words in bold are Possessive Adjectives. We use them to…

a. ◯ indicate that something is near a person.

b. ◯ indicate that something belongs to somebody.

9. Look at the chart and fill in the blanks.

Possessive Adjectives							
Subject Pronouns	I	You			It		You	They
Possessive Adjectives	My		His	Her		Our		

Don't forget! Possessive Adjectives go before the noun!

10. Complete the sentences with Possessive Adjectives.

The students are at the International School doing different things.

a. They are writing _____ addresses.

b. Paula is studying _____ lesson.

c. Jim is doing _____ homework.

d. My friend Chris and Susan are tidying up _____ school things.

e. And I am helping _____ friends.

LISTEN AND SPEAK

1 Listen and check. What is the audio about?

a. ◯ Studying abroad.

b. ◯ Domestic tourism.

2 Now, listen to the testimonial of three students and circle the correct words.

a.

Rebecka Hillbertz
Hometown: Tyringe, Sweden
Study abroad: Perth, Australia

I chose to study abroad so that I could **improve/experience** my English, but also to experience how it is to live in another country and be a part of that **country/culture**.

b.

Estefania Perez
Hometown: Zulia, Venezuela
Study abroad: Arkansas, United States of America

Coming to the United States changed the way that I see the **world/school**, the way that I see people, the way that I accept, interact and really form relationships with people that are **happy/different** from who I am.

c.

Yuki Iwasaki
Hometown: Kyoto, Japan
Study abroad: Perth, Australia

Some people might go studying abroad for, like, landmarks or beautiful… Something **good/beautiful** or food or culture or subjects, something… But for me a friend is the biggest and favorite part of life **studying/traveling** abroad.

Available at: <www.youtube.com/watch?v=-pxi3Ro5UL0>. Accessed on: Feb. 11, 2019.

3 Check the correct answer, based on the students' testimonials.

a. ◯ For all of them, studying abroad is something positive.

b. ◯ Improving the English language is the only reason to study abroad.

c. ◯ In the students' opinion, there are many negative points in studying abroad.

4 In pairs, ask each other: What is your opinion about studying abroad?

5 Imagine you are a new student at school. Stand up in front of the class and introduce yourself, considering these points:

a. Full name
b. Age
c. Favorite school subject
d. City of origin
e. Country of origin

PRONUNCIATION CORNER

1 Listen and practice the tongue twister.

10 A: One-one was a race horse.
B: Two-two was one too.
A: One-one won one race.
B: Two-two won one too.
A: Yo-Yo was a race horse.
B: Yu-Ri was one too.
A: Yo-Yo won one race.
B: Yu-Ri won one too.

2 Practice the sounds.

11 One-one was a race horse.
Two-two was one too.
One-one won one race.
Two-two won one too.
Wow, race horse winners really want rice right away.
Yes, race horse winners really want rice right away.
Right away, right away!

READ AND WRITE

1 Look at the text below. It's…

a. ◯ a recipe.

b. ◯ a job description.

c. ◯ an application form.

2 Erick wants to attend a school year in Melbourne, Australia. He filled up an application form with his personal information to join the Youth Exchange Program.

WELCOME!

Youth Exchange Program

Application Form

Attach a recent, good-quality color photo of yourself. Size: 2 × 2 in. (5 × 6.5 cm)

1. Applicant Information

Full Legal Name as it appears on Passport or Birth Certificate (use all capital letters for your FAMILY name)	Preferred Name	Gender
Erick FISCHER	Erick	◯ Male ◯ Female

Home Address
78, Kaiserdamm Street

City/State	Postal Code	Country
Berlin/Brandenburg	10621	Germany

Home Phone	Cell Phone	E-mail
030 48304033	030 80912988	erick.fischer07@hellomail.com

Date of Birth (e.g. 01/Jan/2006)	Place of Birth (City, State)	Citizen of (Country)
09/Mar/2007	Berlin, Brandenburg	Germany

2. Parent/Legal Guardian Information

Full Name of Father/Legal Guardian	Full Name of Mother/Legal Guardian
Kurt Fischer	Helena Suarez Fischer
Occupation	Occupation
administrator	makeup artist

TWENTY-ONE 21

3 Read the sentences and write **T** (true) or **F** (false) based on the application form.

   a. ( ) A photograph is required.
   b. ( ) The content of the application form is all about Erick's future career plan.
   c. ( ) The e-mail address is an irrelevant information to the Australian school.
   d. ( ) The school wants Erick's parent's phone number to call him/her monthly.

4 Complete the sentences using the words from the box and learn more about forms.

   | clear and concise | logical | purpose | online | questions |

   a. Forms present _____ sequence.

   b. There are _____ or paper forms.

   c. In forms, _____ are usually direct.

   d. The layout of forms can vary according to their specific _____.

   e. Forms are _____ so the form-filler can understand them easily.

5 Are you a bookworm? In pairs, create an application form for the school library. Follow the steps.

   a. Select the items from activity 2 that are necessary to include in a school library form.
   b. Consider new items that can be important for a school library.
   c. Write a draft in your book and show it to your teacher. Make all the necessary adjustments.
   d. Write a final version of your application form in a sheet of paper.
   e. Ask colleagues to fill in your application form. You have to fill in their form too.

TIPS FOR LIFE

Be a nice person

1 Read the text and underline three items you consider most important to maintain a peaceful coexistence in a homestay family.

HOMESTAY FAMILY

It's not easy to live with a homestay family. In day-by-day situations, we need calm and patience. Here are some tips for students who are going through this experience:

- Learn how to greet local people and use "please" and "thank you" in every situation.
- Get to know your host family: where they work/study, what they like to do at their spare time and their preferences.
- Let your homestay family know about you, your preferences, habits, some health problem or dietary restrictions.
- Observe the family routine and try to adapt to it.
- Keep your room always clean and organized.
- Be punctual at your commitments.
- Respect all the cultural differences.
- Avoid conflicts by having honest conversations.

2 In pairs, write down two more tips for a peaceful coexistence in a homestay family. Use a dictionary if necessary.

CHECK YOUR PROGRESS	😃	😐	☹️
Benefits of studying abroad/School subjects			
Present Continuous tense			
Wh- question words			
Possessive Adjectives			
Listening			
Speaking			
Reading			
Writing			

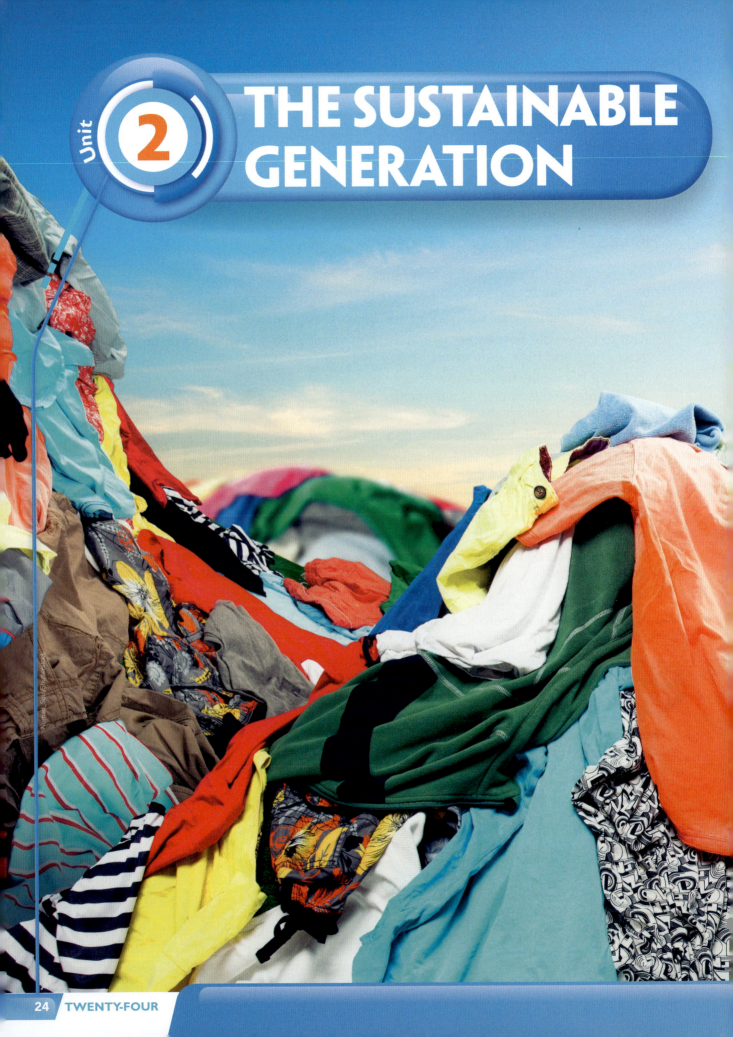

Unit 2: THE SUSTAINABLE GENERATION

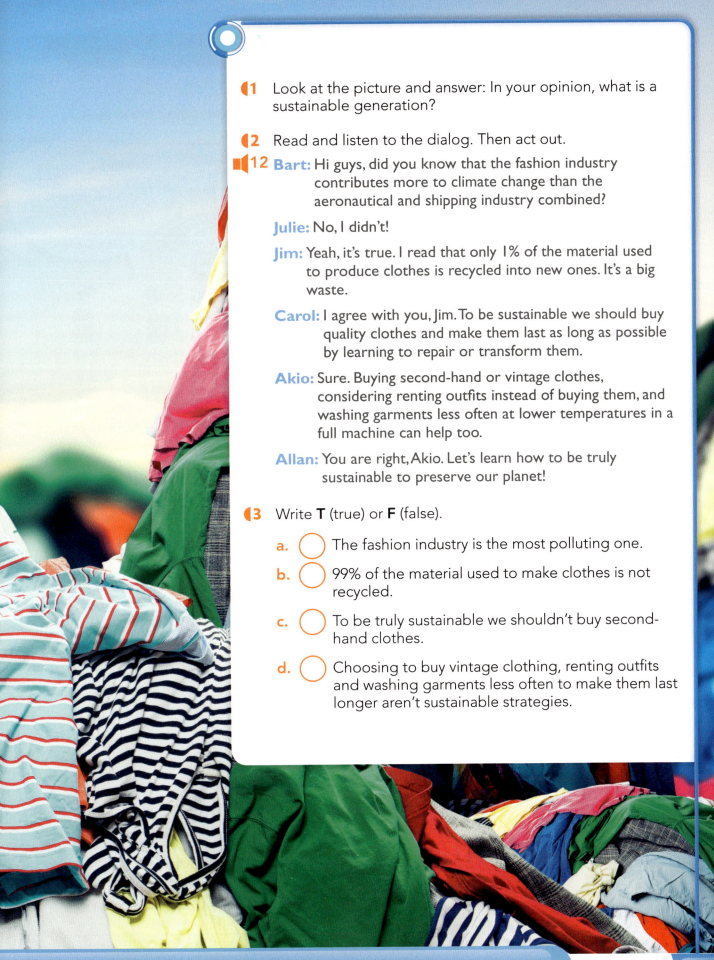

1 Look at the picture and answer: In your opinion, what is a sustainable generation?

2 Read and listen to the dialog. Then act out.

12 Bart: Hi guys, did you know that the fashion industry contributes more to climate change than the aeronautical and shipping industry combined?

Julie: No, I didn't!

Jim: Yeah, it's true. I read that only 1% of the material used to produce clothes is recycled into new ones. It's a big waste.

Carol: I agree with you, Jim. To be sustainable we should buy quality clothes and make them last as long as possible by learning to repair or transform them.

Akio: Sure. Buying second-hand or vintage clothes, considering renting outfits instead of buying them, and washing garments less often at lower temperatures in a full machine can help too.

Allan: You are right, Akio. Let's learn how to be truly sustainable to preserve our planet!

3 Write **T** (true) or **F** (false).

a. ◯ The fashion industry is the most polluting one.

b. ◯ 99% of the material used to make clothes is not recycled.

c. ◯ To be truly sustainable we shouldn't buy second-hand clothes.

d. ◯ Choosing to buy vintage clothing, renting outfits and washing garments less often to make them last longer aren't sustainable strategies.

THINKING AHEAD

1 Read the comic strip and choose the alternative that best completes the sentences.

> Would you like to go to the mall, Chen?

> Yes, George! Do you need to buy anything?

> Actually, I don't need anything. But I would like to buy a new pair of sneakers for the party on Saturday.

> OK, there is a great store there called "Save a Penny". You can buy nice clothes, accessories and shoes for a cheap price.

> It sounds good! I really want to save money for the summer camp. I don't want to spend all my allowance on a pair of sneakers.

> You bet! Let's go there.

a. Two friends are talking about… ○ going shopping. ○ going to the movies.

b. George wants to buy… ○ some clothes. ○ a pair of sneakers.

c. "Save a Penny" has… ○ expensive prices. ○ cheap prices.

d. George wants to… ○ pay any price for a new pair of sneakers. ○ save some of his money.

2 Read the sentence from the comic strip and explain its meaning.

"Actually, I don't need anything. But I would like to buy a new pair of sneakers for the party on Saturday."

_____

3 Read and check.

a. I go shopping…
○ every week. ○ sometimes. ○ rarely. ○ never.

b. I usually spend my money on…
○ clothes. ○ electronics.
○ going out with friends. ○ other things.

4 Do you consider yourself a sustainable consumer? Why (not)?

_____

A WORD WORK

 Listen and repeat.

a shirt

b tie

c blazer

d dress

e pants

f shoes

g blouse

h skirt

i boots

j underpants

k panties

l sweater

m shorts

n bra

o socks

p cap

q T-shirt

r jacket

s jeans

t sneakers

TWENTY-SEVEN 27

12 Look at the second-hand store below. What would you like to buy? Choose five items and complete the following chart.

Your choice	Price
Total amount	

TIME FOR A GAME

Let's play **Hangman**, **Scrambled Words** or **Sausage Game**!

FOCUS ON LANGUAGE

1 Read the cartoon and check the correct alternatives below.

© Betsy Streeter/CartoonStock

GRAMMAR HELPER

Go to page 151.

a. According to the cartoon, the girl...

- ◯ wears medium size.
- ◯ wears large size.
- ◯ is between sizes.

b. "Marge" is...

- ◯ a word she invented to explain her size.
- ◯ *margem.*

c. The action is in the...

- ◯ simple past.
- ◯ simple present.

2 Read the chart and write the following sentences in the interrogative and in the negative forms.

Simple Present								
Affirmative			**Negative**			**Interrogative**		
I	**wear**	jeans.	I	**don't**	**wear** jeans.	**Do**	I	**wear** jeans?
You			You				You	
He	**wears**		He	**doesn't**		**Does**	He	
She			She				She	
It			It				It	
We	**wear**		We	**don't**		**Do**	We	
You			You				You	
They			They				They	

a. Mary likes to buy in second-hand stores.

_____

_____

b. We need to learn how to become sustainable.

_____

_____

c. Jack saves all his allowance.

_____

_____

d. They wear clothes made from recycled materials.

_____

_____

3 Now go back to activity 2 and choose the best sentence to label each image below.

a.

_____

b.

_____

4 Read the dialog below. Then act out.

Salesperson: Can I help you?

Customer: Yes. I'd like a coat, please.

Salesperson: What size are you?

Customer: I'm small.

Salesperson: What color would you like the coat?

Customer: I'd like a gray one.

Salesperson: OK. So you want a small gray coat, is it correct?

Customer: Yes, it is. How much is it?

Salesperson: It's $29,99.

5 Now, in pairs, write two new dialogs using the information from the box and practice them.

| blazer | medium | blue | skirt | large |
| yellow | $13,50 | much | $19,99 | |

_____
_____
_____
_____
_____
_____
_____

6 Brian and Amanda are renting some clothes in a clothes library. In pairs, ask and answer questions about the clothes' prices using **this**, **these**, **that** or **those**. Follow the example below.

How much is **that** dress?
It's $13.00.

a. _____

b. _____

c. _____

d. _____

e. _____

CROSS CULTURAL

A clothes library is a new shopping concept that allows people to shop or borrow clothes, save money and reduce waste and pollution. It's a library that lends clothes instead of books. The garments are second-hand so whether you choose to buy or borrow them, it will still be 100% sustainable.

7 Unscramble the words and make sentences.

a. doesn't/a/Jane/have/dress/yellow/.

_____

b. boots/expensive/are/those/?

_____

c. sweater/green/costs/that/dollars/twenty/.

_____

d. comfortable/I/clothes/prefer/to/wear/.

_____

e. fashion/in/clothes/are/customized/.

_____

LISTEN AND SPEAK

1 In pairs, look at the picture and answer the questions.

a. What is the girl in the picture doing?

b. You are going to listen to a conversation of some kids organizing a donation project. What items do you think the kids will donate?

2 Listen to the dialog about the donation project and complete the gaps.

🔊 14

Bart: Hi, guys! Are you ready for the Donation Project?

Julie: I am! My bag is full of colorful _____ and _____. Look, this is my favorite red _____. It is small for me now. And that blue _____ is a little old, but it is beautiful.

Kitty: They are very nice, Julie. I have a box with _____, shoes, _____ and _____. These ones are new, but I don't like black sneakers. I prefer to wear white ones.

Jim: No problem, Kitty. I am sure someone likes black ones. I have some _____ from my mom. They are too large. And that green and yellow _____ and the brown _____ are from my dad. They want to donate, too.

Bart: It's a great idea! My box has some _____ and _____.

Carol: I have some small _____ and bras. They are all new. I need medium ones. These are small ones.

Jim: Whose are those awesome _____?

Akio: They are mine. I have a collection from Japan.

Carol: Japan? Really? How much are they?

Akio: It doesn't matter, Carol. I want to donate my caps to make other kids happy!

Allan: You are right, Akio. Let's do some good things for people in need and feel happy about it!

Everybody: Yeah! Our Donation Project is the best!

THIRTY-THREE 33

3. Match the columns to complete the sentences.

   a. The kids are organizing... ( ) for people in need and feel happy about it!
   b. Akio wants to donate... ( ) colorful dresses and skirts.
   c. Julie's bag is full of... ( ) his Japanese caps.
   d. Allan wants to do some good things... ( ) a Donation Project.

4. Read the questions and share your answers with your classmates. Then imagine you are one of the characters from the dialog in activity 2 and role-play it creating your own donation project.

   a. Do you usually donate things?
   b. What kind of things do you usually donate?
   c. Where do you take your donations to?

PRONUNCIATION CORNER

1. Listen and say the tongue twister.

   15 **A:** The salesperson sells sneakers,
   Suits and socks, skirts and shirts,
   Shorts and sweaters, shoes and shells.
   B: The salesperson sells stockings,
   Bracelets and earrings, dresses
   and hats. Small shorts and small sweaters.
   A e B: Sneakers and socks,
   Skirts and shirts,
   Shorts and sweaters,
   Shoes and shells, she sells!

Nik Neves/Arquivo da editora

2. Listen to the words in the box. Identify their "s" sound and write them in the right
16 column.

| small shorts | small sweaters | shorts and sweaters |
| sneakers and socks | skirts and shirts | shoes and shells |

/ʃ/	/s/

34 THIRTY-FOUR

READ AND WRITE

1 Look at the picture in activity 2, read the title of the text and answer the questions.

   a. What is the text about?
   b. What is the relation between the picture and the theme of the text?

2 Read the text and check the correct statements.

iCollectClothes

| Donate now | Our Partner Charities | Donation info | Gallery | Blog | Contact us |

Clothes Donation to Charity

Giving a clothes donation to charity also helps the environment. 350,000 tonnes of unwanted clothing goes to landfill every year in the UK according to WRAP. So the more clothing you donate to charity, the less will end up being thrown out as rubbish, and this can only be a good thing.

Donating clothes to charity is cool because it's a win-win situation but the thought of having to carry big bags to a charity shop can be off-putting. Don't worry though, because iCollectClothes has the answer!

Clothes donation couldn't be simpler or more convenient with its unwanted clothes collection service. No longer do you have to trek to a charity shop or remember to put the charity collection bag outside your front door on the right day. iCollectClothes offers an easier way to support good causes. It picks up donations from your door, letting you choose which charity you want to donate to, and a collection date that suits you, while iCollectClothes takes care of the rest.

Available at: <https://www.icollectclothes.co.uk/blog>.
Accessed on: Feb. 4, 2019.

a. ◯ In the UK 350,000 tonnes of unwelcome clothing doesn't go to landfills every year because of donation.

b. ◯ When you contribute to charity you also contribute to sustainability.

c. ◯ People sometimes don't go to charity bazaars because they don't like them.

d. ◯ iCollectClothes is a different kind of donation bazaar.

e. ◯ iCollectClothes picks up donations from your door, letting you choose which charity you want to donate to, and a collection date that suits you.

f. ◯ A blog is a regularly updated website or webpage through which a writer or even a group of writers share texts, images, videos etc.

3 Read the words related to blogs and circle the ones you know. Then look up the meaning of the words you don't know and write them down.

a. post _____

b. scroll bar _____

c. likes _____

d. comments _____

e. toolbar _____

f. header _____

g. subscribe _____

h. recent posts _____

i. follow us _____

j. terms of use _____

4 Imagine you have a blog. Write and publish a text to invite people to visit a clothes library bazaar you are promoting at your school.

163

5 Now share your post with your classmates and teacher.

TIPS FOR LIFE

Donate!

1. Read the poster and answer the following questions.

   a. What is this poster about?

   b. In your opinion, what do the symbols presented in the poster represent?

2. Match the words to their definitions.

   a. Charity   b. Saving   c. Volunteer   d. Help   e. Give   g. Donate

   ◯ tending or serving to save; rescuing; preserving; compensating; redeeming.

   ◯ to […] cooperate effectively with; aid; assist; to save; rescue; to make easier or less difficult; contribute to; facilitate.

   ◯ to present as a gift, grant, or contribution; make a donation of, as to fund or cause; to make a gift, grant; give; contribute.

   ◯ generous actions or donations to aid the poor, ill, or helpless; something given to a person or persons in need; a charitable act or work.

   ◯ to present voluntarily and without expecting compensation; to hand to someone.

   ◯ a person who voluntarily offers himself or herself for a service or undertaking; a person who performs a service willingly and without pay.

   Available at: <https://www.dictionary.com>. Accessed on: Feb. 2, 2019.

CHECK YOUR PROGRESS

	😀	😐	☹️
Clothes			
Adjective order			
Simple Present (Review)			
How much…?			
Listening			
Speaking			
Reading			
Writing			

THIRTY-SEVEN 37

REVIEW UNITS 1 AND 2

1 Complete the sentences using the Present Continuous.

a. Adam _____ some coffee and milk for breakfast. (drink)

b. My aunt's cat _____ a mouse around the house. (chase)

c. Carly and Steven _____ dinner at their favorite Japanese restaurant. (have)

d. Michael _____ my cell phone to call his mother. (use)

e. It _____ a lot in London today. (rain)

2 Now, rewrite the sentences from activity 1 in the negative and interrogative forms.

a. _____

b. _____

c. _____

d. _____

e. _____

3 Read the sentences and underline the correct Possessive Adjectives.

a. Whose sweater is that, mom? That is Lisa's sweater. That is **her/their** new sweater.

b. Why is John so upset now? Because he broke **her/his** expensive computer.

c. We are in the city of London. **Its/Your** historical monuments are beautiful.

d. Here is Mr. Carlyle. He is **his/our** new History teacher.

4 Lisa is talking about her family. Read the text and complete the gaps with the correct verb form.

My name is Lisa Johnson. I _____ (live) with my parents in Melbourne, Australia. My mother's name is Rose, and my father's name is Charles. I _____ (have) one brother and one sister. I usually _____ (wake up) at 6 a.m. and my dad _____ (drive) me to school every morning. My brother and sister are twins and they _____ (go/negative) to school because they are still babies. We _____ (have/negative) a babysitter, so my mother _____ (look) after them every day.

5 Read the questions about Lisa's family and check the correct answers.

a. Does Lisa have a small family?
○ Yes, she does. ○ No, she doesn't.

b. Does Lisa live in Melbourne, Australia?
○ Yes, she does. ○ No, she doesn't.

c. Does Lisa's father drive her to school in the morning?
○ Yes, he does. ○ No, he doesn't.

6 Read the dialog between a customer and a salesperson and put it in order.

(1) Can I help you, sir?

○ OK. What size do you wear?

○ I will pay with credit card.

○ Yes, we do. Here it is... a medium blue shirt.

○ Yes, please. I would like to buy a shirt for work.

○ I wear medium size. Do you have this shirt in blue?

○ It's perfect. I will take it. How much is it?

○ Can I try it on?

○ It's $19,99. Would you like to pay with credit card or in cash?

○ Yes, you can try it on. Follow me, please.

Unit 3: CAN I HAVE THE MENU, PLEASE?

1 Look at the picture and talk to your classmates.

   a. What does the food in the picture represent?
   b. Do you know what healthy food and junk food mean?
   c. Is it important to have a healthy and balanced diet? Why (not)?

2 Read and listen to the dialog. Then act out.

🔊 17 **Liz:** John, do you want to cook dinner for us tonight?

John: Not really, I prefer to order from a restaurant.

Liz: OK! But let's have something healthy, I don't want to eat any junk food.

John: I agree with you. What about some soup or a salad?

Liz: Soup or salad? I don't know… I want something different.

John: Well, let's see… Hamburger and French fries are junk food, pizza is not so healthy either, and you don't want soup or salad… What about Japanese food?

Liz: Great idea! Japanese food is delicious! Let's order some seafood and cooked vegetables. But nothing fried, OK?

John: Yes! Let's order now! And, what would you like to drink?

Liz: Some natural juice will be perfect! No soda today!

John: That's a healthier choice! What a special healthy dinner!

Liz: It sure is, John.

3 Answer the questions according to the dialog.

   a. What kinds of food does John suggest for dinner?
   _____

   b. According to the dialog, are hamburgers and French fries healthy food?
   _____

   c. What do John and Liz decide to eat?
   _____

   d. What would Liz like to drink?
   _____

FORTY-ONE **41**

THINKING AHEAD

1 Read the text and answer the questions.

Do you know what the word brunch means?

The word brunch is a combination of two words. The "br" comes from the word breakfast and "unch" comes from the word lunch. Restaurants usually serve brunch during the weekend from 9:00 a.m. to 2:00 p.m. It is like you're having a late breakfast and an early lighter lunch at the same time.

Where did brunch come from? Some food historians believe brunch originated in England during people's hunt breakfast since 1890s. They usually ate big meals with meats people hunted that day, eggs, chicken livers, bacon, fresh fruits and sweets. Brunch became popular in the United States in the 1930s.

Nowadays a very brief list of food that is served in a brunch consists in bagels, biscuits, sausage, cereal, cinnamon rolls, cupcakes, eggs (fried or scrambled), omelettes, muffins, French toast, potatoes, roasted meat, steak and eggs, ham and eggs, pancake with maple syrup, Belgian waffles, salads, seafood, smoked salmon, soups, fresh fruit, yogurt etc.

Based on: <https://www.mashed.com/22358/brief-history-brunch/>. Accessed on: April 29, 2019.

a. What does **brunch** mean?
___

b. When and where did it start?
___

c. What kinds of food are served during brunch? List some of them.
___
___

d. What time do people usually have brunch?
___

2 Read the text again and list, in your notebook, the mentioned food you consider healthy. Then, tell your classmates why you chose them.

WORD WORK

1. Listen and repeat the menu items. Then classify them using the words from the box.

main course   beverages   appetizers   desserts

tossed salad | Caesar salad | tomato soup

spaghetti and meatballs | grilled chicken and mashed potatoes | fish and chips

ice cream | apple pie | chocolate cake

orange juice | lemonade | soda

2 Search for the words that complete the following paragraph.

```
S O P O T T S O M A J F
S C N D W O R A N G E P
P A M A M M T O L D A D
M E A T B A L L S U P A
Y S U M I T O P A F A D
R A N G S O Y C M I M S
S R O P E M W A K S R O
T A N I O R G K A H E D
M N I J U I C E O T A A
```

The Browns are at Sam's Restaurant to have lunch. They are ordering _____ salad, _____ and chips, spaghetti with _____ and _____ soup. To drink, Kitty wants _____ juice, Liz wants apple _____ and John and the boys want _____. For dessert, they want chocolate _____ and ice cream.

3 Imagine you want to order a meal online and fill in the delivery service form.

www.hello!teens.com/delivery-service

Tom's Meal Delivery Service

Name	Phone number
Address	
Zip Code	

Your Order

Appetizer
Main Course
Dessert
Beverages

Let's play **Bingo** and **Communicative Game**!

44 FORTY-FOUR

FOCUS ON LANGUAGE

1 Read part of the dialog from page 41 again: What do the expressions in blue have in common? Talk to your classmates.

Liz: John, do you **want to cook** dinner for us tonight?

John: Not really, I **prefer to order** from a restaurant.

Liz: OK! But let's have something healthy, I don't **want to eat** any junk food.

2 Read the sentences and complete the chart below.

Simple Present (verb + to + verb)			
Affirmative			
I/You	like		
He/She/It	_____	to eat	fruit for breakfast.
We/You/They	_____		

Negative

I **don't like to eat** fruit for breakfast.

She **doesn't** _____ fruit for breakfast.

Interrogative

_____ you **like to eat** fruit for breakfast?

_____ Olivia _____ fruit for breakfast?

There are verbs which are followed by **to + infinitive** when used in a sentence with other verbs. Some of them are: like, want, prefer, love, hate, need, start, begin, forget, wish, prepare, come, choose, hope, promise etc.
Ex.: I need **to** change my eating habits.; I forgot **to** bring my yogurt.

3 Complete the text about Susan's routine using the correct form of the verbs given.

Susan is a very busy girl. She _____ (get up) at 7 o'clock every day. From 8 a.m. to 3 p.m., she _____ (study) at Prime School and has lunch there. She _____ (not/have) classes on the weekends. On Saturdays, she _____ (like/cook), but sometimes she _____ (prefer/go) to a restaurant with her family. On Sundays, Susan and her family go to the club. She _____ (play) volleyball there, her favorite sport, but her brothers _____ (not/like) it, they prefer basketball. At night, Susan reads good books before bedtime. She _____ (want/be) a literature teacher.

4 Read the comic strip and answer.

a. The toothpick is for... ◯ Jimmy Five.   ◯ Chuck Billy.   ◯ the waiter.

b. Circle the word from the comic strip that indicates who needs the toothpick.

5 Look at the chart and complete the following sentences with the correct pronouns.

Subject Pronouns	I	you	he	she	it	we	you	they
Object Pronouns	me	you	him	her	it	us	you	them

a. _____ is cooking dinner. (him/he)

b. The spaghetti seems delicious. Let's try _____. (he/it)

c. Gloria is doing homework. Do you want to help _____? (her/she)

d. _____ passed the examination. (they/them)

6 Complete the dialog with the correct object pronouns.

Sayuri: Let's make some juice. The oranges are in the fridge. Get _____, please.
Leo: OK!

Sayuri: Is Jim going to eat with _____ (Leo, Carol and me)?

Carol: No, his mother took _____ (Jim) to the dentist.
Sayuri: Carol is preparing the salad. Can you help _____, Leo?
Leo: Sure! I need that tomato. Sayuri, can you get _____ for me, please?

Go to page 152.

7 Read the questions and unscramble the answers.

a. Do the boys always have lunch with Leo?
boys/have/no/the/him./lunch/never/with

No, the boys never have lunch with him.

b. Does Sayuri usually go to the restaurant with you?
usually/yes/she/us./with/goes

Yes, she usually goes with us.

c. Can you help Sayuri cook Japanese food?
I/yes/can/her./help

Yes, I can help her.

d. Do you like to go to the movies with your friends?
I/no/don't/to go/like/them./with/to the movies

No, I don't like to go to the movies with them.

8 Read the chart below and answer the questions.

Would + like		
Interrogative	**Would you like** to have lunch with us?	What **would you like** to eat for lunch?
Affirmative	Yes, **I would**.	**I'd like** some spaghetti with meatballs.
Negative	No, **I wouldn't**.	**I wouldn't like** to eat spaghetti, so I want fish and chips.

a. What would you like to eat for dinner?

b. Would you like to have dinner in a Japanese restaurant?

c. Would you like to eat brunch food?

d. What kind of food would you like to eat every day?

9 Make some invitations using **would** + **like**. Read the question below as an example.

> Would you like to have lunch?

a. have dinner _____

b. play volleyball _____

c. watch an action movie _____

d. have some coffee _____

10 Read the dialogs and complete them using **Do you** or **Would you**.

a.
> **Anna:** _____ like to have some cookies?
>
> **Luke:** Yes, please. I love cookies!

b.
> **Peter:** _____ have dinner at seven o'clock?
>
> **Greg:** No, I don't. I have dinner at eight thirty.

c.
> **Tom:** I don't like Japanese food, I'm sorry.
>
> **Lisa:** That's ok! _____ like to have lunch somewhere else?

d.
> **Karen:** _____ like fried chicken and mashed potatoes?
>
> **Bob:** Yes, I do. It's my favorite kind of meal.

11 Now, complete the sentences with your personal preferences.

a. I like to _____.

b. I prefer to _____.

c. I want to _____.

d. I don't like to _____.

e. I hate to _____.

LISTEN AND SPEAK

1 Listen to Mike and his friends and check the correct answers.

🔊 19

a. They are talking about…
   - ⭕ eating out.
   - ⭕ ordering food online.
   - ⭕ eating at home.

b. They would like to eat…
   - ⭕ healthy food.
   - ⭕ junk food.
   - ⭕ Japanese food.

c. The food they mentioned was:
   - ⭕ fish
   - ⭕ steak
   - ⭕ tuna sandwich
   - ⭕ chips
   - ⭕ grilled chicken
   - ⭕ chocolate cake
   - ⭕ salad
   - ⭕ tomato soup
   - ⭕ mashed potatoes

2 Listen to the dialog again and complete the chart.

🔊 20

	Food preferences	How much is it?
Jen		
Mike		
Lucy		
Tim		

FORTY-NINE 49

3 Now, read the questions below and talk to a classmate.

a. What is your favorite kind of food?
b. What is your favorite type of restaurant?
c. What is the most important thing when choosing a restaurant to eat out?
d. Does your family usually eat out or order food online?
e. What kind of food would you like to order from a restaurant?
f. Do you like to try new kinds of food?
g. Do you always eat vegetables?
h. Do you drink water every day?

4 Read the dialog and practice with a friend. Then finish it orally.

John, do you want to cook dinner for us tonight?

No, I don't. I prefer to...

PRONUNCIATION CORNER

1 Listen and act out the tongue twister.

Peter Piper picked a peck of pickled peppers.
Did Peter Piper pick a peck of pickled peppers?
If Peter Piper picked a peck of pickled peppers,
Where's the peck of pickled peppers Peter Piper picked?

2 Listen and practice the words.

pie	play
price	peppers

READ AND WRITE

1. Skim the text and check the elements you find in it.

   a. ◯ Prices.
   b. ◯ Pictures of food.
   c. ◯ Food suggestions
   d. ◯ Ingredients of the dishes.
   e. ◯ Main meals of the day.
   f. ◯ Servings (amount of food).

2. According to your answers in activity 1, the text is a...

   ◯ menu from a restaurant.   ◯ suggested menu for a healthy diet.

3. Now, scan the menu and write **T** (true) or **F** (false).

HEALTHY MEALS: ONE-DAY MENU

Breakfast
Eating breakfast helps you start your day with plenty of energy.
- One medium bran muffin
- One serving turkey breakfast sausage
- One orange
- One cup non-fat milk
- One cup black coffee or herbal tea

Snack
A mid-morning snack is totally optional. If you eat a larger breakfast, you may not feel hungry until lunchtime.
- One banana
- Glass of water
- One cup plain yogurt with two tablespoons of honey

Lunch
Lunch is often something you eat at work or school, so it's a great time to pack a sandwich or leftovers that you can heat. Or, if you buy your lunch, choose a healthy clear soup or fresh veggie salad.
- Chicken breast (6-ounce portion), baked or roasted
- Large garden salad with tomato and onion with one cup croutons, topped with one tablespoon oil and vinegar
- Glass of water

Snack
A mid-afternoon snack is also optional. Eat just enough to keep you from feeling too hungry because dinner is just a couple of hours away.
- One cup (about 30) grapes
- Glass of water or herbal tea

Dinner
Mentally divide your plate into four quarters. One-quarter is for your meat or protein source, one-quarter is for a starch, and the last two-quarters are for green and colorful vegetables or a green salad.
- One fish fillet
- One cup green beans
- One cup brown rice
- One small garden salad with two tablespoons salad dressing
- Sparkling water with lemon or lime slice

Snack
A light complex carbohydrate-rich evening snack may help you sleep but avoid greasy foods or foods high in refined sugars.
- One cup cottage cheese
- One fresh peach

Based on: <https://www.verywellfit.com/an-example-of-a-healthy-balanced-meal-plan-2506647>.
Accessed on: Jan. 27, 2019.

---

a. ◯ Breakfast is not as important as the snack after lunch.
b. ◯ Water is an important beverage in this menu.
c. ◯ A light complex carbohydrate in the last snack of the day may help you sleep.
d. ◯ Eating sugary food gives you energy during the day.

4 Do you think you can have better eating habits? In pairs, do some research and talk to your teacher, friends and family members about their healthy eating habits. Take notes and write a one-day menu. Follow the steps.

   a. Consider the three main meals and the snacks of the day and write down healthy food items for each one of them.
   b. Give options to replace some ingredients, if necessary.
   c. Mention the benefits of your menu.
   d. Write a draft in your notebook and show it to your teacher. Make all the necessary adjustments.
   e. Write a final version of your menu in your book.
   f. Present your menu to your classmates.

5 In groups, compare your menu with your classmates'. Which suggestions can you give them to make their menus healthier?

TIPS FOR LIFE

Making the right choice

1 In pairs, look at the picture and talk about the title. Then read the text.

> *Super Size Me* is an American documentary related to eating habits. Morgan Spurlock is its protagonist and director.
>
> He talks about his experience of eating at McDonald's for breakfast, lunch and dinner during 30 days.
>
> The result of his experience is that junk food can increase body diseases such as high blood pressure, high cholesterol and diabetes.
>
> According to the documentary, nearly 100 million Americans are today overweight or obese.
>
> Obesity is now, after smoking, the major cause of preventable death in America - more than 400,000 deaths per year. Each day, one in four Americans visits a fast-food restaurant.
>
> Based on: <https://www.imdb.com/title/tt0390521/>.
> Accessed on: Jan. 27, 2019.

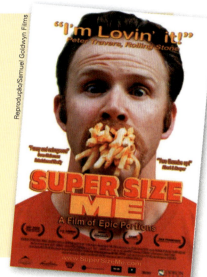

2 What was Morgan's main goal: criticize people who consume a lot of junk food or companies that produce junk food? Discuss in pairs.

3 Now talk about your eating habits.

   a. What kind of food do you usually eat?

   b. What kind of food do you never eat?

   c. What do you eat sometimes?

   d. What's your favorite food?

CHECK YOUR PROGRESS	😃	😐	☹️
Food/Meals			
Simple Present (Verb + to + infinitive)			
Subject/Object Pronouns			
Listening			
Speaking			
Reading			
Writing			

Unit 4 ENJOYING ART

1 Look at the picture. What is the place in it?

2 Read and listen to the dialog. Then act out.

23 **Teacher:** Here we are, kids! This is the Metropolitan Museum of Art! We're going to see famous paintings, sculptures and artworks in general... Now tell me: who likes artworks?

Kitty: I do! I love paintings. When I was a little girl I couldn't paint with brushes, so I used my hands. Now, I can!

Sayuri: Can we take pictures of the artworks, Ms. Jones?

Teacher: Yes, you can, but no flashes, please.

Kitty: Why can't we use flash?

Teacher: Because flashes can damage the paintings.

Kitty: Okay, Ms. Jones. No flashes.

Carol: Where are Renoir's paintings?

Teacher: They are in the next room.

Sayuri: What is Renoir's painting style?

Teacher: It is called Impressionism.

Sayuri: I love his style!

Teacher: Can you paint a picture in Renoir's style?

Sayuri: No, I can't.

Teacher: How about we all try? There is a special room on this floor where we can paint!

Kitty: Great! Come on, Sayuri, I'm sure you can do it.

Sayuri: OK, Kitty. I'll give my best.

3 Write **T** (true) or **F** (false).

a. ◯ The teacher and the students are in the Metropolitan Museum of Art.

b. ◯ Kitty could paint with brushes when she was a little girl.

c. ◯ Students can't use flash to take pictures in this museum.

d. ◯ Renoir's painting style is Impressionism.

THINKING AHEAD

1 Besides the museum mentioned in the dialog, in which of the places below is it possible to appreciate art and cultural events?

a. ◯ Movie theater   b. ◯ Theater   c. ◯ Cloth stores

2 Now, read the text and check the answers.

http://www.salasaopaulo.art.br

THE SALA SÃO PAULO

The Sala São Paulo, considered to be the best concert hall in Latin America, was inaugurated in 1999, in the former headquarters of the Sorocabana Railway Company, a historical heritage building in São Paulo that dates from 1938. [...]

The mobile acoustic lining, consisting of 15 free-standing panels, makes it possible to alter the volume inside the concert hall, adjusting the acoustics to fit each performance [...]. Each feature of the Sala São Paulo hall was designed to make it one of the best and most beautiful venues in the world, which harmoniously brings together history, technology and the arts. [...]

Nilton Fukuda/Agência Estado

CONCERT HALL

With its reputation as one of the most beautiful concert halls in the world, Sala São Paulo has a world-class acoustic design for the performance of diverse symphonic works and chamber pieces. [...]

Available at: <http://www.salasaopaulo.art.br/paginadinamica.aspx?pagina=espacosparaeventos&Cultura=en-GB>.
Accessed on: Jan. 28, 2019.

a. What kind of art can a person appreciate in Sala São Paulo?

◯ music concerts   ◯ dance performances   ◯ art exhibitions

b. A concert hall is, essentially, a place where...

◯ dance performances take place.

◯ art exhibitions take place.

◯ concerts of classical music take place.

3 In pairs, do some research and write definitions, in Portuguese, for the expressions below. Share with your classmates and teacher.

a. symphonic works

b. chamber pieces

A WORD WORK

1 Listen to the audio and check your preferences. 🔊 24

MUSIC

○ classical music ○ pop music

LITERATURE
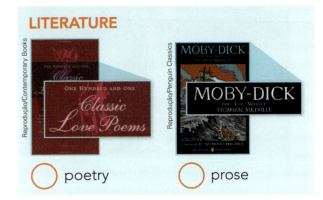
○ poetry ○ prose

SCULPTURE

David, by Michelangelo. *Flamingo*, by Alexander Calder.

○ classical ○ modern

PAINTING

Madonna of the carnation, by Leonardo da Vinci *Merry Structure*, by Wassily Kandinsky, 1926

○ classical ○ modern

DANCE

○ classical ballet ○ modern ballet

THEATER

○ comedy ○ tragedy

CINEMA

○ fiction ○ non-fiction

2 Look at the pictures and complete the sentences with words from the box.

| classical | poetry | pop | sculptures | comedy | modern |

She can't play classical music, but she can play _____ music.

The boys and girls are at the theater. They are watching a _____ movie.

The girl is having a _____ ballet class.

What is the man reading?
He is reading _____.

Can this painter paint in a classical style?
Yes, he can, but he prefers painting in a _____ style.

There are some interesting _____ in this museum.

TIME FOR A GAME

Let's play **Hot Potato** and **What's missing?**.

FOCUS ON LANGUAGE

1 Read some fragments of the dialog from page 55 and answer the questions.

Kitty: I do! I love paintings. When I was a little girl I couldn't paint very well. Now, I can paint. [...]

Sayuri: Can we take pictures of the artwork, Ms. Jones?

Teacher: Yes, you can, but no flash, please.

Kitty: Why can't we use flash?

a. In "I can paint" the modal verb **can** indicates...
   - ○ permission in the affirmative form, in the present.
   - ○ ability in the affirmative form, in the present.

b. In "When I was a little girl I couldn't paint very well", the modal verb **could** means...
   - ○ be able to in the past.
   - ○ be able to in the present.

c. To make the negative form of the modal **can/could** we use...
   - ○ the modal can/could + the main verb + not.
   - ○ the modal can/could + not + the main verb.

d. In "Can we take pictures of the artworks, Ms. Jones?", **can** is used to...
   - ○ ask permission.
   - ○ indicate ability.

e. To make the interrogative form of the modal **can/could**, we use...
   - ○ can/could + subject + main verb.
   - ○ subject + can/could + main verb.

Go to page 154.

Modal Verb	
Can (present)	**Could (past)**
General ability I **can** play the drums	General ability I **could** play the drums when I was younger.
Ask for permission (informal) **Can** I borrow your brush to paint a picture, please?	Ask for permission (polite) **Could** I use your brush to paint a picture, please?
Make requests **Can** you help me, please?	Make requests (polite) **Could** you pass me the crayons, please?
Possibility It **can** be difficult to paint this mural.	Suggestion (when asked what to do) We **could** go to the exhibition if you like.
Offer to help someone **Can** I carry these books for you?	

12 Check the correct answer to complete the sentences.

a. I'm sorry, but I _____ go to Phil's concert next Friday.
   ○ can   ○ can't   ○ couldn't   ○ could

b. Julie was sick yesterday. She _____ dance.
   ○ can   ○ can't   ○ could   ○ couldn't

c. Please, sing louder! We _____ hear you very well.
   ○ could   ○ couldn't   ○ can   ○ can't

d. Selena was a smart child. She _____ play the piano when she was three.
   ○ couldn't   ○ can   ○ could   ○ can't

e. It's sunny outside. _____ we go to the rock concert?
   ○ Could   ○ Couldn't   ○ Can   ○ Can't

f. Peter is a great actor. He _____ act very well.
   ○ could   ○ couldn't   ○ can   ○ can't

g. The museum is closed. We _____ go there today.
   ○ can   ○ could   ○ can't   ○ couldn't

h. I'm not in a hurry. I _____ wait for you if you need more time to finish your poem.
   ○ could   ○ can   ○ can't   ○ couldn't

13 Read the sentences from the box, then write what you **can** or **can't** do.

| touch the paintings   look at the paintings and sculptures |
| talk about the paintings and sculptures with my classmates   take pictures using flash |

In a museum...	
I can	I can't

4 Read the sentences from the chart. Then complete the gaps with the correct **Wh- question.**

Wh- questions			
Why can't she go to the museum? Because she is studying.	**What's** her name? Her name is Tarsila do Amaral.	**Where** are the students? They're in the museum.	**Who** is he? He's Vincent van Gogh.

why   what   where   who

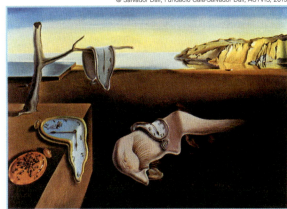

a. _____ is this painter? He is Salvador Dalí.

b. _____ can I see his sculptures in this museum? You can see them in the Central Room.

c. _____ is the most famous Dalí's painting? It is *The Persistence of Memory*.

d. _____ is Salvador Dalí famous? Because he was a great surrealist artist.

The Persistence of Memory by Salvador Dalí, 1931.

5 Put the words in the correct order to make questions. Then give personal answers.

a. studying/are/why/you/?

A: _____

B: _____

b. Theater is/Municipal/the/where/?

A: _____

B: _____

c. your/number/is/what/phone/?

A: _____

B: _____

d. class/is/when/art/your/?

A: _____

B: _____

6 Match the questions to the answers.

> Who is this painter?   Where is he from?   Why isn't she painting in a classical style?
> What is this?   Who is this actor?   Where is this building?

a.

_____

It is in Sydney, Australia.
It is the Opera House, a multi performing arts center.

b.

_____

He is Tom Hanks, an American actor and filmmaker. He won an Oscar for his famous film *Forrest Gump*.

c.

_____

He is Salvador Dalí. A Spanish Catalan painter born in Figueres, Spain. Dalí was best known for the bizarre images in his surrealist work. His best-known work was *The Persistence of Memory*. Dalí's artistic repertoire included film, sculpture, and photography.

d.

_____

This is a modern sculpture created by Tomie Ohtake in Santos, São Paulo, in 2008. It is a 15-meter tall steel sculpture, painted with automotive paint and weighs 60 metric tons.

e.

_____

Because she likes Modern Art. The term is usually associated with art in which the traditions of the past have been thrown aside in a spirit of experimentation. It's closely related to Modernism.

f.

_____

João Carlos Martins is a Brazilian pianist and conductor. He is from São Paulo and he is known worldwide.

LISTEN AND SPEAK

1. Music is one of the most popular languages of art. What music style do you like? Who are your idols? Why? Share with your classmates.

2. Listen to two fans talking about their idols. Then complete the chart.

Her name is _____.

She was born in _____.

She can...
- ◯ sing.
- ◯ write songs.
- ◯ act.
- ◯ play the flute.

Her name is _____.

She was born in _____.

She can...
- ◯ sing.
- ◯ make sculptures.
- ◯ act.
- ◯ dance.

3. In pairs, talk about what your idols **can** or **can't** do.

4 Now, it is your turn to talk about what you can do. Look at the picture and use examples from the box to talk to your classmates about what you can and can't do.

| act in a movie   act in a musical (play)   dance   sing   paint |
| write a song   draw   write books |

PRONUNCIATION CORNER

1 Listen and act out the jazz chant.

Jazz Chant

A: **Can** aunt Peggy paint?
B: Of course she **can**.
A: She **can** paint very well.

A: **Can** the boys play baseball?
B: Of course they **can**.
A: They **can** play very well.

A: **Can** the girls play basketball?
B: Of course they **can**.
A: They **can** play very well.

A: **Can** you help me, Jill?
B: No, I **can't**.
A: Of course you **can't**.

2 Listen and say if the sentences are in the affirmative or in the negative form.

LANGUAGE TIPS

- In the affirmative and interrogative forms, we pronounce **can** as /kən/.
- In short answers, we pronounce **can** as /kæn/.

READ AND WRITE

1 Look attentively at the picture of a mural by Eduardo Kobra, a Brazilian artist. Check what you can notice in it.

a. ◯ There is a predominant color.
b. ◯ The painting looks flat and the man has no movement.
c. ◯ The predominant color relates to the theme of the mural.
d. ◯ It's not possible to identify any specific details in the mural.

TO LEARN MORE

Street art is a form of art expression that we can find in the streets, especially in urban areas. The artist paints on the wall or create their art expression at any other permanent surface outdoors.

2 What do you feel when you look at Kobra's mural? Talk to your classmates.

3 Read about Kobra's mural and, in pairs, answer the questions that follow.

---

www.hello!teens.com/Kobra

THE LARGEST STREET ART MURAL IN THE WORLD

(1) This mural is an artistic work by one of the most known current street art muralists, Eduardo Kobra. He was born on January 1st, 1976, in Brazil. Kobra usually utilizes bright colors and bold lines linking a kaleidoscope theme throughout his art.

This mural is considered the largest mural of the world and it is located in São Paulo, Brazil, –a chocolate company's facade, at Castello Branco Road, km 35.

It's a 5.742 m² space recognized by The Guinness and it reproduces the Brazilian Amazonia cocoa harvest scene.

The mural is 30 meters high and 200 meters wide. He used a total of 3.2 thousand cans of spray and many liters of paint.

(5) The artist, who brings a striking trait in his style, with geometric characteristics and utilizes strong and vibrant colors, portrays a young multicolored man sailing in a canoe loaded with cocoa over a chocolate river.

There is also an image of the fruit *in natura* dripping chocolate still in its liquid state giving us the idea of the river stream.

There is also the representation of a big chocolate bar in the back of the masterpiece that involves many drawings.

Kobra, beyond his geniality, made a stunning representation of the cocoa as a typical and authentic Brazilian piece of culture, through this street art.

Based on: <https://www.ebiografia.com/eduardo_kobra/>; <https://www.guiadasemana.com.br/na-cidade/galeria/murais-do-kobra-em-sao-paulo-que-voce-precisa-visitar-o-quanto-antes>. Accessed on: Feb. 13, 2019.

a. What are the main characteristics of Kobra's murals?

b. How high and wide is his mural?

c. Which paragraphs describe the mural?

d. Which paragraph informs the location of the mural?

e. Pay attention to some adjectives used to refer to Kobra and to describe his mural. Do they express a positive, neutral or negative view of the work of art?

4 Consider Kobra's work and the neighborhood you live in. Then reflect on the questions:

a. Where would you like to produce a mural or any other type of street art?

b. What message could your work of art convey?

5 Draw a sketch of your artwork on your notebook. Remember to consider where you would like it to be and the message in it.

6 Show your sketch to a classmate and talk about each other's piece of art. Then write a description of your classmate's work. Follow the instructions below.

a. Listen to your classmate's explanation.

b. In your notebook, write a description of your classmate's artwork.

c. Be sure that your description answers the questions below:
- Who is the artist?
- Where is he/she from?
- Where is the artwork located?
- What are its main characteristics?
- What message does it convey?

d. Show your description to your teacher and make all the necessary adjustments.

e. Write a final version of this work description.

7 Present your classmate's work to the whole class and read your description out loud.

Part of collaborative mural by Brazilian artists OSGEMEOS, Nina Pandolfo, Nunca, Finok and Zefix, at 23 de Maio Avenue, São Paulo, 2008.

TIPS FOR LIFE

Talents and Skills

1 Think about the questions below and discuss them with your classmates.

a. In your opinion are people born talented or are they trained to develop their talents and skills?

b. Do you know your skills and talents? Would you like to develop some talent? Which one?

c. Do you know people close to you who are very skilled or talented at something? Explain.

d. Do you know people who use their talents to help others? Give examples.

2 Interview your classmates or family. Ask what they **can** or **can't do**. Then fill in the chart.

	Sing	Dance	Play an instrument	Play sports	Paint	Surf
Now it's your turn!						

CHECK YOUR PROGRESS	😃	😐	☹️
Art Forms			
Can/Could			
Wh- questions			
Listening			
Speaking			
Reading			
Writing			

REVIEW
UNITS 3 AND 4

1 Complete the conversation with the appropriate object pronouns. Use the clues given to help you.

John: What about going away for the weekend?

Kitty: Can I invite my friend Sayuri to come with _____ (our family)?

Liz: Yes, you can invite _____ (Sayuri) to join us.

Tobby: And what about _____ (Tobby)? Can I invite my friends, too?

John: No, you can't. But we can send _____ (Tobby's friends) some pictures, OK?

Liz: Well, let's pack our bags and put _____ (our bags) in the car.

Leo: First, I need to call Jim and ask for a favor. I will ask _____ (Jim) to take care of Fido while we are away.

Liz: Great! It will be an amazing weekend.

2 Read and match the sentences.

a. I'm thirsty.
b. Would you like to eat pizza?
c. I'd like a cheeseburger, please.
d. Carly would like your help to do the homework.

◯ Would you like to have some fries, too?
◯ Sure. I can help her.
◯ I'd like to drink a glass of water, please.
◯ No, I wouldn't. I prefer to eat sushi.

3 Rewrite the sentences using the verbs in parentheses. Follow the example.

a. Liz has dinner with her friends at an Italian restaurant. (like)
   Liz likes to have dinner with her friends at an Italian restaurant.

b. Kitty and Carol play volleyball at school. (prefer)
   _____

c. Leo stays at home. (want)
   _____

d. I studied for my Math test. (decide)
   _____

4 Choose the correct modal verb to complete the sentences.

a. _____ I offer you a glass of water? You look thirsty.
   ○ Could   ○ Can't   ○ Couldn't

b. _____ I open the door, please? It's hot in here.
   ○ Couldn't   ○ Can   ○ Can't

c. When I was a child I _____ roller-skate, but now I can.
   ○ couldn't   ○ could   ○ can't

d. My grandma _____ speak French well, but she _____ speak English.
   ○ could/couldn't   ○ can/could   ○ can/can't

e. Chris _____ play his new electric guitar well.
   ○ could   ○ can   ○ can't

f. Melinda _____ play table tennis before, but now she _____ play it very well.
   ○ couldn't/can   ○ can't/could   ○ can't/can

g. I _____ sleep last night. It was so hot and humid.
   ○ can   ○ couldn't   ○ could

5 Write the questions using the *Wh-* question words.

a. Why can't I go to the beach today?
   You can't go to the beach today because it's raining.

b. _____
   We can study for the History test this afternoon.

c. _____
   We are from Cambridge, England.

d. _____
   Sayuri's favorite singer is Taylor Swift.

e. _____
   They can't go to the concert because they don't have money.

6 Now, answer: What are you doing now?

_____

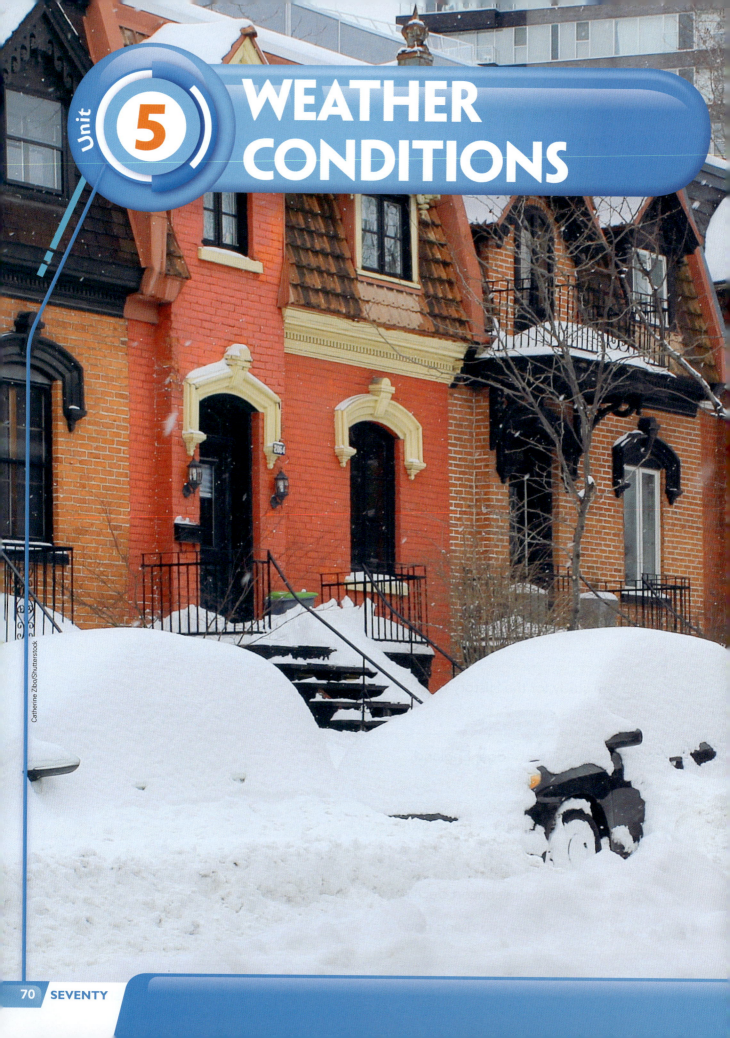

Unit 5: WEATHER CONDITIONS

1 Look at the picture and talk to your classmates.

  a. What can you see in this picture?

  b. Have you ever been to a place with bad weather conditions?

  c. Are you afraid of weather phenomena? Why (not)?

2 Read and listen to the dialog. Then act out.

🔊 28

Allan: Where were you last Sunday?

Leo: I was in Honolulu, Hawaii, for the weekend. And you?

Allan: I was in Chicago, at grandma's. Were you alone in Honolulu?

Leo: No, I was with my family.

Allan: What was the weather like?

Leo: It was warm and sunny. The temperature was about 83 °F.

Allan: Lucky you! There was a winter storm in Chicago during the weekend.

Leo: A winter storm? How bad was it?

Allan: It was snowing too much and the temperature was below 32 °F.

Leo: Oh! It was freezing!

Allan: Grandma was scared, so we stayed home.

Leo: And what was the day like?

Allan: It was cold, so I spent all of my time watching TV and drinking hot chocolate!

Leo: It sounds nice!

3 Write **T** (true) or **F** (false).

  a. ◯ Allan spent the weekend in Honolulu, Hawaii.

  b. ◯ Leo was in Honolulu, Hawaii, for the weekend.

  c. ◯ The temperature in Hawaii was 83 °F.

  d. ◯ There was a winter storm in Chicago.

  e. ◯ Allan was at the mall with his grandma during the winter storm.

THINKING AHEAD

1 In pairs, look at the picture and read the text.

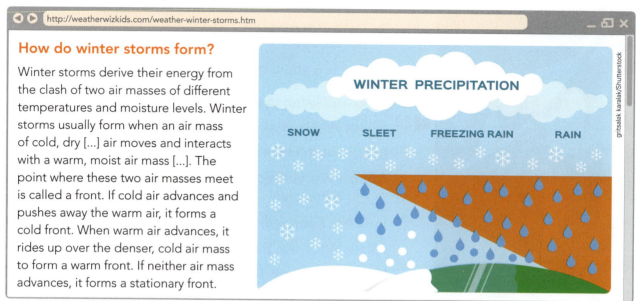

How do winter storms form?

Winter storms derive their energy from the clash of two air masses of different temperatures and moisture levels. Winter storms usually form when an air mass of cold, dry [...] air moves and interacts with a warm, moist air mass [...]. The point where these two air masses meet is called a front. If cold air advances and pushes away the warm air, it forms a cold front. When warm air advances, it rides up over the denser, cold air mass to form a warm front. If neither air mass advances, it forms a stationary front.

Available at: <http://weatherwizkids.com/weather-winter-storms.htm>. Accessed on: Feb. 12, 2019.

2 Complete the sentences according to the text above.

a. The clash of two air masses usually forms _____.

b. _____ is what we call the meeting point of two air masses.

c. _____ storms are formed when cold, dry air mass interacts with _____, moist air mass.

3 What is the temperature? Read the text and convert Celsius into Fahrenheit.

What is temperature?

Temperature is a degree of hotness or coldness that can be measured using a thermometer. It's also a measure of how fast the atoms and molecules of a substance are moving. Temperature is measured in degrees on the Fahrenheit, Celsius, and Kelvin scales.

a. 30 °C = _____ °F

b. −10 °C = _____ °F

c. 15 °C = _____ °F

Available at: <http://weatherwizkids.com/weather-temperature.htm>. Accessed on: Feb. 14, 2019.

To use a Fahrenheit to Celsius converter online, go to: <www.unitconverters.net/temperature/fahrenheit-to-celsius.htm>. Accessed on: Feb. 12, 2019.
To convert Celsius into Fahrenheit you can multiply the temperature by 9, then divide by 5, then add 32. For more information, go to <www.mathsisfun.com/temperature-conversion.html>. Acessed on: Feb. 13, 2019.

A WORD WORK

1 What is the weather like? Listen and say.

🔊 29

a. It's sunny in Goiânia, GO.
b. It's rainy in São Paulo, SP.
c. It's windy in Fortaleza, CE.
d. It's foggy in Curitiba, PR.

e. It's snowy in São Joaquim, SC.
f. It's cloudy in Belo Horizonte, MG.
g. It's humid in Manaus, AM.
h. It's chilly in Caxias do Sul, RS.

Seasons

It's summer, the sun is shining.
It's fall, the leaves are falling.
It's winter, it's cold.
It's spring, I can see flowers everywhere.

Temperature

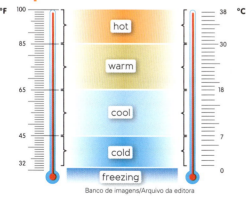

TO LEARN MORE

Snowflakes are made of six-sided ice crystals. They are formed in clouds where the temperature is below freezing. As the snow crystals grow, they become heavier and fall toward the ground.

Based on: <http://weatherwizkids.com/weather-winter-storms.htm>. Accessed on: Feb. 5, 2019.

2 Use the weather information from activity 1 and answer: what is the weather like in your city now? It's _____.

3 Look at the chart and answer the following questions.

Weather Chart

Mexico City 78 °F

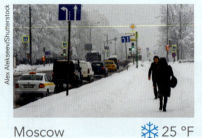
Moscow ❄ 25 °F

	sunny
	cloudy
	snowy
	partly cloudy
	rainy

Rio de Janeiro 87 °F

London ☀ 35 °F

4 What is the weather like in…

a. Mexico City? _____
b. Moscow? _____
c. Rio de Janeiro? _____
d. London? _____

5 Complete the month sequence and answer: what month are we in?

a. _____ d. _____ g. July   j. _____
b. February   e. May   h. August   k. _____
c. _____ f. June   i. _____ l. December

6 What is the weather like in the months listed below according to each city? In pairs, do some research and answer the questions.

a. January in London: _____
b. February in Rio de Janeiro: _____
c. March in California: _____
d. October in Toronto: _____

Let's play **The Alphabet Game** and **Spelling Bee**!

FOCUS ON LANGUAGE

1 Read these sentences from the dialog on page 71 and check the correct answer.

> **Allan:** Where **were** you last Sunday?
> **Leo:** I **was** in Honolulu, Hawaii, for the weekend. And you?

a. ○ In the sentences "Where **were** you last Sunday?" and "I **was** in Honolulu" the verb **to be** is in the past tense.

b. ○ In the sentences "Where **were** you last Sunday?" and "I **was** in Honolulu" the verb **to be** is in the present tense.

c. The expression "last Sunday" indicates…

○ that the action started and finished in the past.

○ that the action still continues.

2 Read the charts with the Simple Past of the verb **to be** and some Simple Past Expressions.

Verb To Be – Simple Past

Affirmative			Negative			Interrogative		
I	was	at home yesterday.	I	wasn't	at home yesterday.	Was	I	at home yesterday?
You	were		You	weren't		Were	you	
He	was		He	wasn't		Was	he	
She			She				she	
It			It				it	
We	were		We	weren't		Were	we	
You			You				you	
They			They				they	

Simple Past Expressions

last night/Tuesday/week/month/year

ten minutes **ago**/two hours **ago**/five days **ago**

yesterday morning/afternoon/evening/night

Go to page 156.

3 Based on the first chart in activity 2, complete the dialog with the Simple Past of the verb **to be**.

Samuel: Where _____ you last Saturday?

Martin: I _____ at a barbecue at Bob's house.

Samuel: _____ you alone?

Martin: No, my brother Tony _____ with me.

Samuel: _____ Tom there?

Martin: No, he _____, Samuel.

Samuel: What _____ the weather like?

Martin: It _____ hot and sunny.

Samuel: _____ the barbecue good?

Martin: Yes, it _____ great!

4 Identify the places and complete the texts with the words from the box.

| about   were (2×)   spring   summer   winter   hot   fall |
| was (5×)   beautiful   snowy   temperature   weather |

a. It _____ _____ in Brazil last January. It _____ very _____ and the _____ was about 37 °C in Salvador, BA.

b. Holambra is a city in São Paulo state. I _____ there in September. It _____ _____ at the time. There _____ a lot of colorful flowers. They _____ very _____.

c. Last year in July, during _____, it was _____ in Gramado, RS. The temperature was _____ 0 °C.

d. In the _____, I _____ in Curitiba, PR. The _____ was cold and rainy in April.

5 Read the chart Simple Past Expressions in activity 2 and fill in the gaps.

a. Today, I'm very happy. _____ I was sad.

b. Carol is in the classroom, now. _____ she was at the mall.

c. My brother slept late _____. He was very tired _____.

d. My parents traveled to Australia _____.

6 Read the dialog between Avery and Mila.

Where was your brother last Saturday?

He was at the mall.

7 Write other dialogs with the information suggested. Then practice with a classmate.

a. Thomas/last Wednesday/dentist

_____
_____

b. Claire/yesterday afternoon/Carol's birthday party

_____
_____

c. Karen and Daniel/yesterday evening/Chinese restaurant

_____
_____

d. you/last Monday night

_____
_____

8 Read the chart with some prepositions of time.

In	On	At
in January	on Thursday	at 9:30
in 2012	on July 1st, 2018	at midnight
in summer	on Friday morning	at night
in the morning/afternoon/evening	on the weekend (American English)	at Christmas/Halloween at the weekend (British English)

9 Choose the correct preposition of time and fill in the gaps. Explain why.

a. I was in Belém _____ March. _____
   ○ on   ○ at   ○ in

b. Let's go to Mercado Ver-o-Peso _____ Sunday. _____
   ○ in   ○ on   ○ at

c. I was at Porto das Docas _____ 8 o'clock yesterday evening. _____
   ○ at   ○ in   ○ on

d. My family and I were in the Modern Museum of Art _____ Saturday.
   _____
   ○ on   ○ in   ○ at

LANGUAGE TIPS

On is used to talk about flat surfaces: big and small.
   They walked **on** the field.
   The pen is **on** the desk over there.

At is used to talk about specific locations.
   I met him **at** the supermarket.
   The kids usually have lunch **at** school.

GRAMMAR HELPER

Go to page 157.

LISTEN AND SPEAK

1 Complete the sentences using your own information and practice them with a classmate.

a. Where were you yesterday?

_____

b. What was the weather like?

◯ sunny   ◯ warm   ◯ cold   ◯ rainy

c. How was the temperature?

_____

d. Do you usually check the weather report before leaving home? What for?

_____

_____

_____

e. Where can you find weather reports?

_____

2 Listen to the weather report and focus on the general information: what is it about?
🔊 30

_____

_____

_____

3 Now, listen again and circle the alternatives you hear.
🔊 31

a. The weather for the weekend is going to **change/remain** the same.

b. **Last month/Yesterday** they broke their October temperature record.

c. In Gravesend County the temperature reached **29/39** degrees.

d. In Hawarden the highs reached **28.1/28.2** degrees.

4 In pairs, list possible applications for weather reports.

_____

_____

_____

_____

5 In pairs, match the information from both columns to form a paragraph.

a. Last week, it… ◯ was hot and cloudy.
b. The beaches… ◯ was about 37 °C.
c. The weather… ◯ were very beautiful.
d. The temperature… ◯ was spring time in Brazil.
e. The hotel… ◯ was very comfortable and cheap.

6 In pairs, talk about the following questions. Then write a similar paragraph talking about your last trip and present it to your classmates.

- Where did you go to on your last trip?
- What was the weather like?
- How was the hotel accomodation?

_____
_____
_____
_____
_____
_____
_____

PRONUNCIATION CORNER

1 Listen to the chant and act it out.

32
A: I'm sinking, I'm sinking!
B: Pardon, are you thinking?
A: No, I'm not. I'm sinking in the sea!
B: Pardon, are you sinking in the sea or thinking about the sea?
A: Please, I'm sinking, I'm not thinking, gee!
B: Oh, gosh! A float for him! He's sinking!

2 Listen and say.
33

| thank – sank | sin – thin | pass – math |
| mouth – mouse | sink – think | |

80 EIGHTY

READ AND WRITE

1 Read the fragments in activity 2. Choose the best alternatives.

a. Where were the fragments extracted from?
- ◯ They were extracted from recipes.
- ◯ They were extracted from books.
- ◯ They were extracted from news reports.

b. They are…
- ◯ lead paragraphs.
- ◯ headlines.
- ◯ body.

c. What are their objectives?
- ◯ To catch the readers' attention.
- ◯ To offer basic information about the content.
- ◯ To inform readers about the 5Ws (Who, What, Where, When, Why) of the news report.

2 Read the texts below and answer the questions.

Text 1

https://weather.com

California Storms Trigger Water Rescues, Mudslides: Death Toll Rises to 6

Available at: <https://weather.com/news/news/2019-01-14-california-parade-rain-snow-impacts>. Accessed on: Feb. 14, 2019.

Text 2

https://weather.com

Paris' Famed Eiffel Tower Closes in Snow and Ice

Available at: <https://weather.com/news/news/2019-01-23-france-paris-snow-ice-ei el-tower>. Accessed on: Feb. 14, 2019.

Text 3

https://weather.com

2018 Was Wettest Year on Record in Over Two Dozen Cities in the East, Midwest, Including Washington D.C. and Pittsburgh

Available at: <https://weather.com/news/news/2018-12-15-record-wet-year-2018-washington-dc-baltimore>. Accessed on: Feb. 14, 2019.

a. The texts are all related to a topic. What is it?

___

b. Underline the verbs in the texts above. Which verb tenses were used?

___

c. Is there a period at the end of the texts?

d. Consider your answer to the previous question. Why do you think that happens?

3 In your opinion, which headline is the most interesting? Why?

4 Now, it's your turn to create meaningful and catchy headlines. Follow the steps.

   a) Think of headlines you would like to read in newspapers. What are they about?

   b. Don't forget to:
   - be informative;
   - be objective;
   - use bold capital letters;
   - choose the appropriate verb tense;
   - consider the target audience before choosing the words.

   c. Write a draft and show it to your teacher.

   d. Make all the necessary adjustments.

   e. Write the final version.

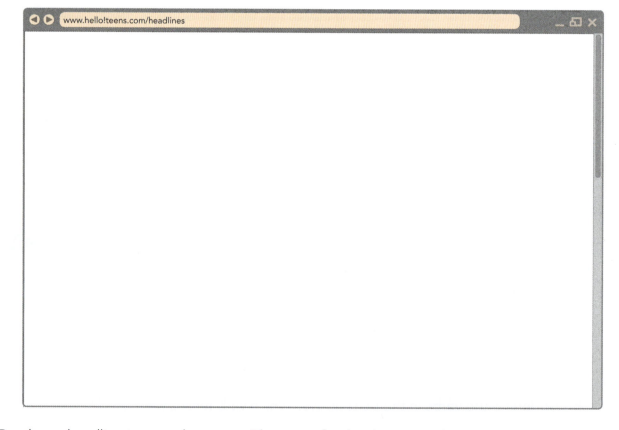

5 Read your headline to your classmates. Then vote for the three most interesting ones.

TIPS FOR LIFE

Climate change

1 Look at the cartoon and discuss with a friend.

a. What does the polar bear want?

b. Why do you think he wants that?

Available at: <www.cartoonstock.com/cartoonview.asp?catref=forn441>. Accessed on: Feb. 14, 2019.

2 Read the quote and discuss it with your classmates.

"The greatest threat to our planet is the belief that someone else will save it."

Robert Swan, British explorer and activist.

Available at: <www.activesustainability.com/environment/robert-swan-and-our-planet/>. Accessed on: Feb. 14, 2019.

3 In your opinion, what can you do to help save the planet? Create a poster with possible actions.

CHECK YOUR PROGRESS	😀	😐	☹️
Weather/Seasons			
To be (Simple Past)			
Prepositions of time			
Listening			
Speaking			
Reading			
Writing			

Unit 6
IT WAS AN AMAZING PARTY!

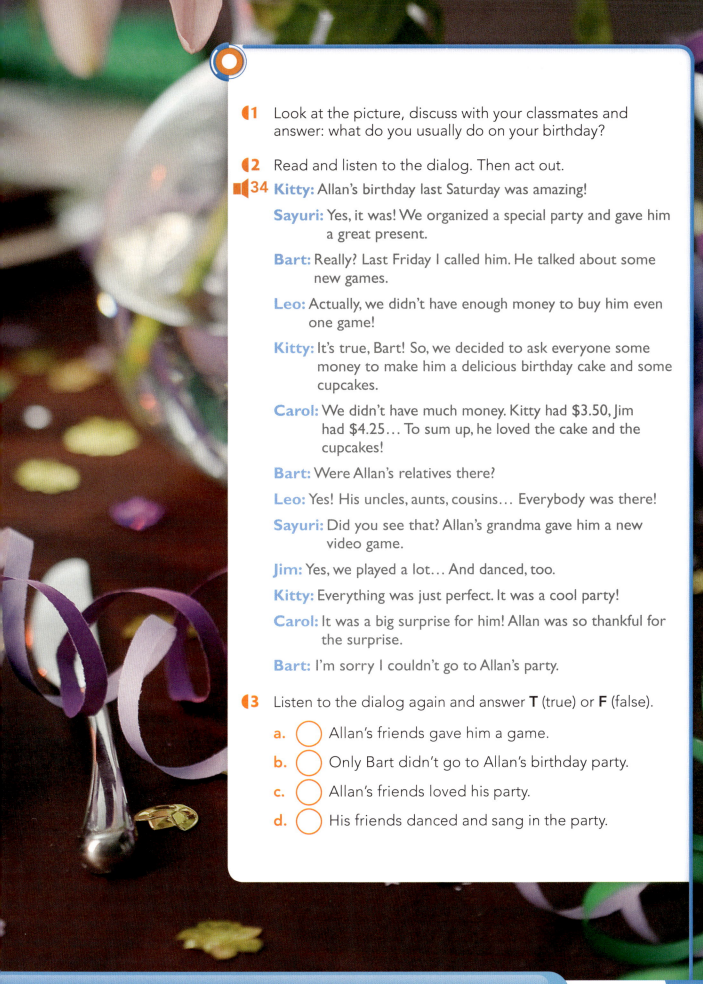

1. Look at the picture, discuss with your classmates and answer: what do you usually do on your birthday?

2. Read and listen to the dialog. Then act out.

34 **Kitty:** Allan's birthday last Saturday was amazing!

Sayuri: Yes, it was! We organized a special party and gave him a great present.

Bart: Really? Last Friday I called him. He talked about some new games.

Leo: Actually, we didn't have enough money to buy him even one game!

Kitty: It's true, Bart! So, we decided to ask everyone some money to make him a delicious birthday cake and some cupcakes.

Carol: We didn't have much money. Kitty had $3.50, Jim had $4.25… To sum up, he loved the cake and the cupcakes!

Bart: Were Allan's relatives there?

Leo: Yes! His uncles, aunts, cousins… Everybody was there!

Sayuri: Did you see that? Allan's grandma gave him a new video game.

Jim: Yes, we played a lot… And danced, too.

Kitty: Everything was just perfect. It was a cool party!

Carol: It was a big surprise for him! Allan was so thankful for the surprise.

Bart: I'm sorry I couldn't go to Allan's party.

3. Listen to the dialog again and answer **T** (true) or **F** (false).

a. ◯ Allan's friends gave him a game.

b. ◯ Only Bart didn't go to Allan's birthday party.

c. ◯ Allan's friends loved his party.

d. ◯ His friends danced and sang in the party.

THINKING AHEAD

1 Look at the picture and answer the questions.

The classmates want to prepare a surprise birthday party for the new student. They are calculating how much money they have.

a. How much money does Ben have? _____

b. How much money does Minori have? _____

c. How much money do Sophia and Bob have? _____

d. How much money do Chris and Rose have? _____

2 Now, look at the chart and check the correct option, considering the money the classmates have.

Birthday Party Supplies		Price
	Candles	$3.99
	Party plates	$7.19
	Plastic forks	$8.58
	Plastic cups	$9.64
	Napkins	$5.99
	Balloons	$6.48
	Candy	$10.10

a. Ben can buy ◯ balloons. ◯ plastic cups.

b. Minori can buy ◯ party plates. ◯ plastic forks.

c. Chris and Rose can buy ◯ candy. ◯ candles.

d. Sophia and Bob can by ◯ napkins. ◯ plastic cups.

LANGUAGE TIPS

In countries like the U.S. and Canada, we use a dot to separate dollars from cents. It's different from Brazil, where we use a comma.

3 Answer the questions below based on the previous activities.

a. How much money do the classmates have together? _____

b. How much money do they need to buy all the party supplies? _____

c. Do they have enough money to buy them? _____

WORD WORK

1 Listen and say.

35 **Let's help Lucy!**

Lucy needs to buy presents for her best friend Michael and her sister Tracy, but she can't make up her mind.

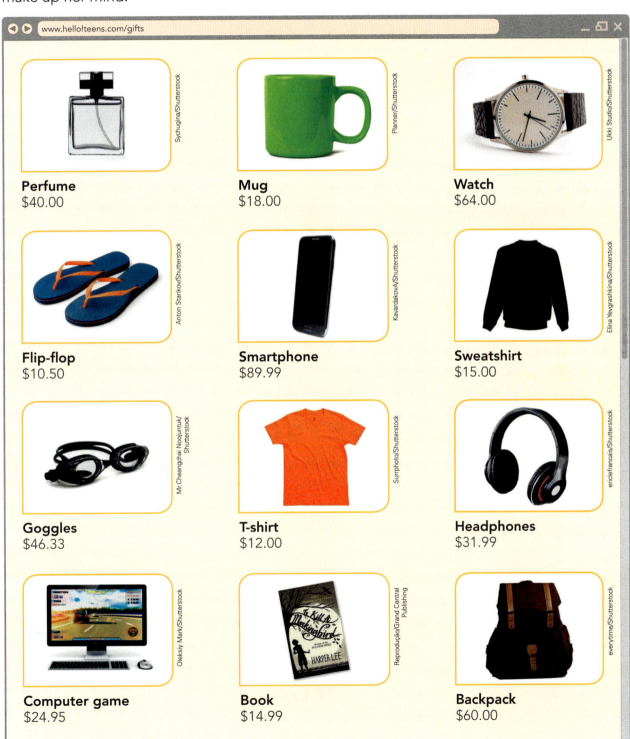

2 Complete the text according to the pictures in activity 1.

For her best friend Michael, Lucy wants to buy a _____, but she is not sure about it. She thinks he prefers a good _____. On the other hand, she knows that he really needs a new _____, but she doesn't have enough money. It's too expensive! And for her sister, Tracy, she wants to buy a nice _____ and a _____.

- How much money does Lucy need to buy her sister's gifts? _____

3 In pairs, break the code and write the missing words. Then practice the mini dialogs.

A	B	C	D	E	F	G	H	I	J	K	L	M
🎁	❄	☺	🏠	📅	✉	🔧	💬	☀	🕐	📎	🔥	♡

N	O	P	Q	R	S	T	U	V	W	X	Y	Z
💣	⭐	📄	🗓	▲	🌞	🔔	🔒	📷	🪄	☕	🔑	💡

a. **A:** Did your brother enjoy his new 🔧⭐🔧🔥📅☺? _____
   B: Yes, he did. He 💣🍎☺⭐🕐📅🏠 them so much. _____

b. **A:** Where did Olivia go 🕐📅☺🔥📅▲🏠🎁🕐? _____
   B: She went to the mall because she wanted to buy new ✉🔥☀📄 - ✉🔥⭐📄☺.
   _____

c. **A:** Which items were on sale last week?
   B: The 🪄🎁🔥☺💬 and the 🔥-☺💬☀▲🔥. _____

d. **A:** Please, use your 💬📅🎁🏠📄💬⭐🍎📅☺ to listen to music. _____
   B: OK, ☺⭐▲▲🕐. _____

Let's play **Scrambled words** and **Word list**!

FOCUS ON LANGUAGE

1 Read part of the dialog from page 85 and circle the correct options.

> **Kitty:** Allan's birthday last Saturday was amazing!
> **Sayuri:** Yes, it was! We **organized** a special party and gave him a great present.
> **Bart:** Really? Last Friday I **called** him. He **talked** about some new games.

a. The sentences are about actions in the **present/past**.

b. We can recognize this verb tense through verbs like **talked/amazing**.

c. In the **past/future** tense, the verbs often end with **-ed/-ing**.

d. Expressions of time, like **present/last Friday**, help to recognize this verb tense, too.

2 Look at the chart and do the following activity.

Simple Past – Regular Verbs						
Affirmative		**Interrogative**			**Negative**	
I			I		I	
You			you		You	
He	planned a surprise party.	Did	he	plan a surprise party?	He	didn't plan a surprise party.
She			she		She	
We			we		We	
You			you		You	
They			they		They	
Examples -ed (Regular Verbs)						

1. **close** – She clos**ed** the store at 6 a.m.
2. **play** – My team play**ed** last Sunday.
3. **marry** – They marr**ied** last month in London.
4. **visit** – I visit**ed** my cousins on the weekend.
5. **stop** – At noon, I stop**ped** to eat something quickly.
6. **open** – The new mall open**ed** its doors yesterday.

- The sentence "We didn't have enough money" is in the _____ form.

  a. ◯ negative   b. ◯ affirmative   c. ◯ interrogative

LANGUAGE TIPS

In British English, we double the last **l** even though the last vowel is not stressed. For example: travel – trave**ll**ed, cancel – cance**ll**ed, level – leve**ll**ed.

13 Complete the text using the past form of the verbs from the box.

plan	decide	invite	play
start	enjoy	finish	

Last Saturday, Allan's friends _____ to plan a surprise birthday party for him. They _____ some of his friends. The party _____ at 5:00 p.m. At 6:00 p.m. they _____ video games and at 7:00 p.m. they _____ a competition. At 8:00 p.m. they _____ the games and sang "Happy Birthday". Allan's friends _____ the party very much.

14 Look at the pictures and complete the sentences using the verbs in the Simple Past.

a.

(stay – play)

A: _____ Mike _____ home yesterday?
B: No, he _____. He _____ basketball all day!

b.

(visit – study)

A: _____ Mariana _____ her friends last night?
B: No, she _____. She _____ last night.

15 Look at the chart and talk to a classmate.

Simple Past – Short Answers	
Did you study yesterday?	
Affirmative	Yes, I did.
Negative	No, I didn't.

Go to page 158.

a. Did you play video game yesterday? _____
b. Did your father watch series on TV last Sunday? _____
c. Did your friends practice any sports? _____

6 Read the sentences. Then check the correct options.

> If you are hungry, there are **some** tuna sandwiches on the kitchen table.
> Do you have **any** brothers or sisters?

a. The quantity of sandwiches and of brothers and sisters is...

○ definite. ○ indefinite.

b. The words that express the ideia of quantity are...

○ some and any. ○ new and there.

7 Look at the chart below and fill in the gaps.

	Affirmative	Interrogative	Negative
Some	There are **some** candles on the table.	—	—
Any	—	Is there **any** orange juice?	There aren't **any** sandwiches.

a. We use _____ in affirmative sentences.

b. We use _____ in interrogative and negative sentences.

Go to page 159.

We use **some** in interrogative sentences when we are offering or requesting something. For example: "Would you like **some** juice or **some** milk?" (*offering*), "Can you give me **some** money?" (*requesting*).

8 Akio is making a chocolate cake for Allan's birthday party. Complete the dialog with **some** or **any**.

Akio: Hello, Aretha!

Aretha: Hello, Akio!

Akio: I'm making a chocolate cake, but I don't have all the ingredients.

I have two eggs, but I don't have _____ milk.

Do you have _____ milk?

Aretha: Sorry, Akio. I don't have _____ milk.

But I have _____ cocoa powder. Would you like some?

Akio: Yes! Thanks, Aretha!

Aretha: You're welcome!

9 Read the chart and do the following activity.

Uncountable	Countable
How much water do you drink every day? • Not **much**. • I drink **a lot of** water every day.	**How many** comic books do you have? • I have **many** comic books. • I have **a lot of** comic books.

- Match the columns to complete the sentences.

    a. We use **many** with… ○ both uncountable and countable nouns.

    b. We use **much** with… ○ countable nouns.

    c. We use **a lot of** with… ○ uncountable nouns.

Go to page 159.

Countable nouns are those that we can count using numbers, therefore they have singular and plural forms. Examples: *candle(s), balloon(s), cup(s)*.
Uncountable nouns are those that we can't count using numbers, so they only have a singular form. Examples: *milk, juice, information*.

10 Read the flyer and answer the questions.

a. How much does the swimsuit for girls cost?

_____

b. How much does the red cap cost?

_____

c. How many shorts can you buy for $13.50?

_____

d. How many pairs of sunglasses can Carol buy for $50.00?

_____

LISTEN AND SPEAK

🔊 **1** Listen and circle the ingredients Carol needs to make the cupcakes for Allan's birthday.
🔊 36

Easy Birthday Cupcakes

cocoa powder

flour

sugar

butter

milk

eggs

limes

strawberries

baking powder

LANGUAGE TIPS

While the **tablespoon** is a big spoon used for measuring or serving food, the **teaspoon** is a small spoon used for mixing tea or coffee in a cup. In cooking, **cup** can be used to measure liquid and dry ingredients.

Based on: <https://dictionary.cambridge.org/>. Accessed on: Feb. 15, 2019.

🔊 **2** Listen and reorder the recipe according to the steps to prepare it.
🔊 37

◯ Mix well.

◯ Add the sugar, the butter and the milk.

◯ Then stir in the all-purpose flour and the cocoa powder.

◯ Finally, add the baking powder and bake it for 40 minutes.

◯ Beat well to mix the flour and cocoa powder.

◯ First, beat the eggs.

NINETY-THREE 93

3 In pairs, create and role-play a dialog using verbs and expressions in the past tense.

Actions	Expression of time
Dance at the party	Yesterday
Visit friends	Yesterday afternoon
Listen to music	Yesterday morning
Plan a trip	Last weekend
Travel to the beach	Last month
Watch TV series	Last year
Play video game	Last semester
Prepare a recipe	Last Monday, Tuesday…

PRONUNCIATION CORNER

1 Listen and practice the jazz chant.

Rose has red hair.
Her hair is long.
Red hair is rare!
Look at her head!
Her head is red.
Her hair is red.
Her hair is rare.
Rose is rare!

2 Practice the sounds.

rat	–	hat
red	–	head
rare	–	hair
rabbit	–	habit
rope	–	hope

3 Listen and repeat the tongue twister.

I know a rat who wears a hat.
I hope I have a rope.
This rabbit has a strange habit.

READ AND WRITE

1 Lucy is planning a surprise for her sister: a chocolate cake! Read the recipe and check the items you can find in it.

a. ◯ Ingredients
b. ◯ Kitchen utensils
c. ◯ Serving size information
d. ◯ Step-by-step instructions

Chocolate Cake

Ingredients

4 eggs
2 cups of sugar
2 tablespoons of butter
2 cups of milk
3 cups of all-purpose flour
3 tablespoons of cocoa powder
1 tablespoon of baking powder

Directions

1. Beat the eggs and add the sugar.
2. Add the butter and the milk. Mix well.
3. Add the flour and the cocoa powder. Beat well for two minutes.
4. Add the baking powder and mix well.
5. Bake for 40 to 50 minutes and the cake is ready!

2 Read the recipe and answer the questions with **Y** (yes), **N** (no) or **NM** (not mentioned).

a. ◯ Does the recipe have a title?
b. ◯ Are the ingredients listed in order of use?
c. ◯ Are directions full of unnecessary details?
d. ◯ Does the recipe present the flavor of the cake?
e. ◯ How much money do we need to make the cake?

For more tips on how to make a cake, go to <www.youtube.com/watch?v=E7D7-HtaTLo>. Accessed on: Feb. 15, 2019.

NINETY-FIVE **95**

3 What is your favorite family recipe? Ask your parents or relatives for a special recipe and take notes in your notebook. Let's create a cookbook with your classmates and share some special recipes.

   a. Choose an easy, but delicious recipe.
   b. Make sure that it has a title, ingredients and directions.
   c. List all ingredients in order of use.
   d. In the directions, write objective sentences and use verbs in the imperative form.
   e. Pay attention to indicate the amounts, otherwise the recipe can go wrong.
   f. Write a draft and show it to the teacher. Make all the necessary adjustments.
   g. If possible, do some research on pictures that can illustrate the recipe.
   h. Write a final version in your book.

TIPS FOR LIFE

Being a conscious consumer

1 In English, there is a saying: "A penny saved is a penny earned". What does it mean? Discuss with a classmate.

2 Now, read the comic strip, talk to a classmate and answer.

a. Did the woman buy necessary things?
_____

b. Did the woman save money? Why (not)?
_____

c. Is the woman a conscious consumer?
_____

CHECK YOUR PROGRESS	😃	😐	☹️
Birthday party supplies and gifts			
Simple Past – Regular verbs			
Some × Any			
How much × How many			
Listening			
Speaking			
Reading			
Writing			

REVIEW
UNITS 5 AND 6

1 Read the text and complete the gaps with **at**, **in** or **on**.

Last summer, Joe went to his grandparents' house. They live in a small town. _____ 2015, they bought a new house in a quiet neighborhood. Now his grandfather works _____ the Internet café. Joe's grandparents were always home _____ night, but now they go for a walk in the town's park every night. _____ the weekends, they usually go to the mall to eat _____ a special restaurant. Joe loves the quiet life of a small town.

2 Give complete and true answers about yourself.

a. Were you at home yesterday evening?
   _____

b. Was your family at the beach last Sunday?
   _____

c. Was your father working yesterday afternoon?
   _____

d. Were you and your friend at school yesterday morning?
   _____

3 Write questions according to the answers.

a. _____
   It was 39 °C in Palmas last night. It was really hot.

b. _____
   She was at the dentist yesterday evening.

c. _____
   It was rainy and cold yesterday in São Paulo.

d. _____
   It was cold and snowy in New York last December.

4 Read the dialog between Allan and his mom. Then, fill in the gaps with **some**, **any**, **many** or **much**.

Allan: Do you have _____ plans for my birthday party, mom?

Mom: Oh, sorry. I don't have _____ yet. What do you have in mind, Allan?

Allan: I would like to have a slumber party. Can I invite _____ of my friends to a sleepover?

Mom: Sure! What would you like to offer them to eat, Allan?

Allan: Is there _____ chocolate ice cream in the fridge?

Mom: Yes, there is _____, I guess. How _____ pizzas can we order?
How _____ orange juice should I buy?

Allan: I don't know, mom... What about a birthday cake?

Mom: Yeah, I can buy that strawberry cake you love so much, son.

Allan: You're the best, mom. Thanks a lot!

5 Read the sentences and circle the correct alternative.

a. Students **didn't visit/didn't visited** the National Museum yesterday. They **played/play** soccer at school.

b. Did the students **enjoy/enjoyed** Allan's slumber party? Yes, they **did/didn't**.

c. Mom and dad **walked/walk** for an hour in the park last Saturday.

d. Did Aline **study/studied** for the test? No, she **did/didn't**. She **get/got**) a low grade.

e. My cousins **watched/watch** an adventure movie last Sunday.

Unit 7 DID YOU KNOW…?

1 Look at the picture and talk to your classmates.

    a. Have you ever had a brilliant idea? Which one?

    b. In your opinion, how does a brilliant idea come up?

2 Read and listen to the dialog. Then act out.

41

Jim: Hi, Allan, come in.

Allan: Hi, Jim, what's up?

Jim: I'm fine. I'm researching some interesting facts for my history homework. It is about great inventions.

Allan: Can I help you?

Jim: Sure! Did you know that the cell phone was invented by Martin Cooper, in 1973?

Allan: No, I didn't. Awesome!

Jim: And one of the first video game consoles was Atari 2600. It had two control paddles.

Allan: I have a file stored in my cloud about great inventions. Check it out: Tim Berners Lee wrote the software for the World Wide Web, the popular "www", in 1990, and it helped revolutionize the internet and make it freely available to the world.

Jim: Cool! Now I understand why we use "www" before any address on the internet.

Allan: That's right.

Carol: Hey, Allan, Kitty and I also have some homework to do. Can you share your files with us, so we can do our research?

Allan: Sure, I can. I am sending them to you right now.

3 Answer the questions according to the text.

    a. Which inventions were mentioned in the dialog?

    _____

    b. What is the meaning of "www"?

    _____

THINKING AHEAD

1 Read about two projects created to make a difference. Then do the following activities.

Projects that improve lives

Brazil joined the Maker Movement last year by hosting the country's first large-scale Maker Faire Rio de Janeiro. […] There were a wide range of maker exhibits, workshops, and talks, and impressively, a good number of them used maker smarts to try and make the world a better place for all. […]

Educational Biochemistry Game

A group of public high school students have developed an educational game to facilitate the learning of complex concepts in biology. This board game, made with recyclable materials, features a table of genetic code, where enzymes try to correct mutations. […]

Smart Cane for the Blind

Thomas Rossi, a graduate student in Product Design at PUC-Rio, has designed Gala, an intelligent cane capable of detecting and reporting the status of traffic signals, in real time, for blind users.

Available at: <https://makezine.com/2018/11/01/8-projects-that-improve-lives-featured-at-maker-faire-rio-de-janeiro/>. Accessed on: Feb. 7, 2019.

TO LEARN MORE

Read the complete news article and watch videos about these projects on: <https://makezine.com/2018/11/01/8-projects-that-improve-lives-featured-at-maker-faire-rio-de-janeiro/>. Accessed on: Feb. 7, 2019.

2 In pairs, answer the questions below in your notebook, according to the text in activity 1.

a. Describe the first invention.

b. Describe the second invention.

c. Which invention did you like the most? Why?

d. How does this invention help society?

A WORD WORK

1. Look at some inventions that helped to make our lives easier.
🔊 42

automobile
by Karl Benz
(Germany, 1885)

airplane
by Alberto Santos Dumont
(Brazil, 1906)

cell phone
by Martin Cooper
(the USA, 1973)

computer
by Charles Babbage
(England, 1830)

camera
by Johann Zahn
(Germany, 1685)

headphones
by Ernest Mercadier
(France, 1891)

television
by John Logie Baird
(Scotland, 1925)

telephone
by Alexander Graham Bell
(the USA, 1876)

video game console
by Ralph Baer
(Germany, 1972)

ONE HUNDRED AND THREE   103

2 Write the inventions from activity 1 in order in the timeline.

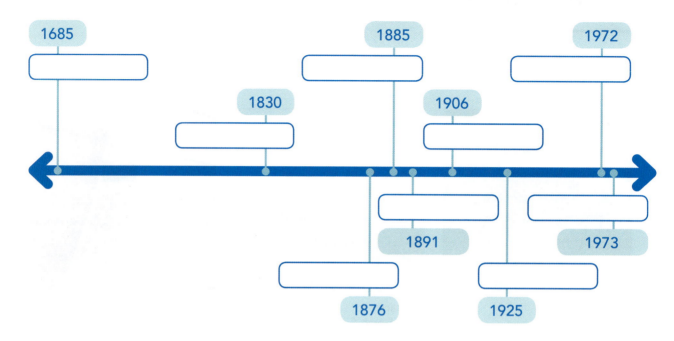

3 Match each invention to its definition and guess the last one.

a. A piece of equipment that is used to talk to someone who is in another place.

b. A vehicle designed for air travel that has wings and one or more engines.

c. A piece of equipment with a screen on the front, used for watching programmes.

d. A piece of electronic equipment for playing games on.

e. A device with parts that cover each ear through which you can listen to something, such as music, without other people hearing.

f. An electronic machine that calculates data very quickly, used for storing, writing, organizing, and sharing information electronically or for controlling other machines.

g. A device for taking photographs, making films, or recording images on videotape.

○ computer

○ video game console

○ airplane

○ headphones

○ telephone

○ television

g _____

Available at: <https://dictionary.cambridge.org>. Accessed on: Jan. 28, 2019.

TIME FOR A GAME

Let's play **Stop!** and **Spelling Bee**.

FOCUS ON LANGUAGE

1 Read the comic strip and check the true sentences.

a. ◯ There are only sentences in the present tense.
b. ◯ "Ma'am" is short for "Mother".
c. ◯ "My dog didn't eat my homework" is a negative sentence.
d. ◯ "He wrote it!" is in the past tense.

GRAMMAR HELPER
Go to page 159.

2 Read the chart below. Then rewrite the sentences in the affirmative or negative form according to the comic strip.

Simple Past – Irregular Verbs						
Affirmative		**Interrogative**			**Negative**	
I			I		I	
You	**ate** a lot last night.	**Did**	You	**eat** a lot last night?	You	**didn't eat** a lot last night.
He/She/It			He/She/It		He/She/It	
We/You/They			We/You/They		We/You/They	

a. Charlie Brown did his homework.

_____

b. Charlie Brown didn't go to school.

_____

c. Snoopy ate Charlie Brown's homework.

_____

d. Charlie Brown didn't tell the teacher who did his homework.

_____

3 Read the sentences about some historical figures and rewrite them in the interrogative form.

a. William Shakespeare became famous for his plays.

___

b. Steven Spielberg won an Oscar for the movie *Schindler's List*.

___

c. Christopher Columbus thought the Earth was round.

___

TO LEARN MORE

- William Shakespeare (1564-1616) was an English poet, playwright and actor. One of his most famous works is *Romeo and Juliet*.
- Steven Spielberg (1946-) is an American director, screenwriter and producer. He is known for directing movies like *ET* and *Jurassic Park*.
- Christopher Columbus (1451-1506) was an Italian explorer who first travelled across the Atlantic Ocean and stumbled upon the Americas.

4 Fill in the gaps with the Simple Past of the verbs in parentheses. Then match the pictures to the sentences.

a. Tom _____ himself while he was washing the dishes. (cut)

b. Monica _____ a cup of tea before going to bed. (drink)

c. William Shakespeare _____ a lot of famous plays. (write)

d. Leonardo da Vinci _____ the famous *Mona Lisa*. (paint)

5 Read about some teenagers who won awards for their inventions and notable actions. Then fill in the gaps using the verbs from the box.

> entered   won   became   held   used   modified   was   experimented   called   lost

EZ Baby saver

Andrew Pelham of Nashville, Tennessee, _____ a kid inventor to do something about saving the lives of young children left in hot cars. The device is made of rubber bands and duct tape which form a strap that stretches across the driver's side of the car from the backseat to the front and attaches to the driver's side door. Parents are reminded that their child is in the backseat when they try to get out of the car. Andrew _____ his kid invention in the Rubber Band Contest for Young Inventors _____ each year in Akron, Ohio, and _____ second place and a $500 prize which he _____ to buy a laptop and create his own website.

Available at: <https://www.stemjobs.com/amazing-kid-inventions/>. Accessed on: Jan. 28, 2019.

Braille

The raised dots system of reading for the blind _____ Braille is named after Louis Braille. He was born in France in 1809 and _____ his sight when he was just 3 years old. While attending the National Institute for Blind Youth in Paris, he _____ with different ways of reading using just touch. He _____ a military code used for reading messages on the battlefield in the dark and went on to invent Braille, making it possible for blind people to read. He _____ just 15 years old.

Available at: <https://www.cbc.ca/kidscbc2/the-feed/kids-have-great-ideas-6-famous-kid-inventions>. Accessed on: Jan. 28, 2019.

6 Read about the automobile history and underline the verbs in the past form.

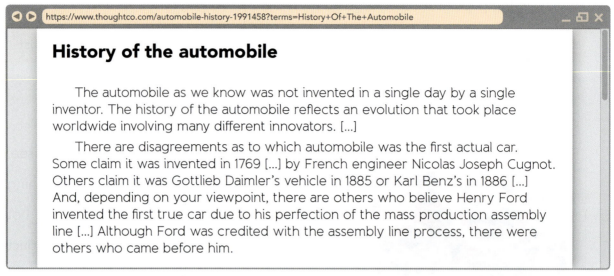

Available at: <https://www.thoughtco.com/automobile-history-1991458?terms=History+Of+The+Automobile>.
Accessed on: Feb. 21, 2019.

7 Now, go back to the text in activity 6 and find sentences with:

a. a regular verb in the Simple Past.

_____
_____
_____
_____

b. an irregular verb in the Simple Past.

_____
_____
_____
_____
_____

8 Use the words below to write sentences in the Simple Past. Follow the example.

a. Henry Ford/invent/the car mass production.

Henry Ford invented the car mass production.

b. John Koss/develop/the first stereo headphones.

_____

c. The computer/begin/with Charles Babbage, an English Mathematics professor.

_____

d. Motorola/produce/the first handheld mobile phone in 1973.

_____

LISTEN AND SPEAK

1 Look at the picture and answer the questions.

Alexander Graham Bell

a. Have you ever heard about Graham Bell? What do you know about him?
_____

b. What was his greatest invention?
_____

2 Now, listen to his short biography and choose the correct answers.

a. Alexander was born on _____ 3rd, 1847.
   ○ February   ○ March   ○ April

b. Eliza was the name of Alexander's _____.
   ○ wife   ○ friend   ○ mother

c. He had _____ brothers.
   ○ two   ○ three   ○ four

d. Graham Bell was _____.
   ○ an engineer and a doctor   ○ a scientist, an inventor and a teacher
   ○ a doctor

3 Listen and match the inventions from the box to the correct pictures.

| bicycle | light bulb | LCD screen display |

Karl von Drais
_____

Thomas Edison
_____

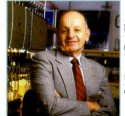

George H. Heilmeier
_____

ONE HUNDRED AND NINE **109**

4 Now, it's your turn. Create a timeline with the important events of your life. Example: the day of your birth, your first spoken word, a nice trip, the first year of school etc. Then present your timeline to your classmates.

PRONUNCIATION CORNER

1 Listen and act out the jazz chant.

🔊 **45**

Did you make a cake?
No, I **made** a pancake.
Did you have a break?
Yes, I **had** a long break.

Did you write a letter?
Yes, I **wrote** a letter.
Did you write it to Bill?
No, I **wrote** it to Jill.

Did you send an e-mail?
Yes, I **sent** an e-mail.
Did you send it to Begail?
Yes, poor Begail is in jail.

2 Listen and say some irregular verbs in the Simple Past.

🔊 **46**
go – went
bring – brought
lend – lent
drink – drank

READ AND WRITE

1 The text below is a biography about Marie Curie. Check the information you expect to find in it.

a. ◯ Her occupation.   c. ◯ Her legacy to the world.
b. ◯ Date of birth and death.   d. ◯ Facts of her personal life.

2 Now, read the biography and check if your predictions were correct.

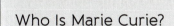

Who Is Marie Curie?

Marie Curie (1867-1934)

Marie Curie was born in 1867 in the city of Warsaw, Poland. Her real name was Maria Sklodowska and her parents were both teachers. Marie got Science training from her father after school. In 1891, when she was 24 years old, she moved to Paris to live with her sister and study Physics and Math. Marie studied at Sorbonne, a famous research public university in Paris. There she began to use the French name Marie.

Then, Marie began to work at the same laboratory as Pierre Curie, a French physicist and a professor. They got married in 1895 and had two children.

She and Pierre, during their investigation of radioactivity, discovered two important chemical elements which were added to the periodic table: polonium and radium.

In 1903, the Curies won the Nobel Prize for Physics along with Professor Henri Becquerel for their research on radiation. This prize brought them fame. She was the first woman to receive this award.

In 1911 Marie Curie was given another Nobel Prize for Chemistry.

Marie died in July 1934 from leukemia caused by overexposure to radiation from her research. She was 66 years old.

3 Find the correct statement according to the text and correct the wrong ones.

a. ◯ Marie Curie and her husband Pierre were French.

b. ◯ The Curies discovered just one chemical element, radium.

c. ◯ In 1903, they were awarded the Nobel Prize for Physics.

d. ◯ Marie Curie died at the age of 67 from natural causes.

4 What is the most surprising fact in Marie Curie's biography? Discuss with a classmate.

5 In pairs, think of some inventions that changed the world. In your opinion, which one is the most revolutionary? Who created it? Discuss with your classmate. Then do some research and write a biography of the inventor.

    a. Before writing, reflect on these questions:
- How does this person influence people's lives?
- Were there relevant facts in his/her life? Which ones?
- When was he/she born?
- Is he/she dead? If so, since when?

    b. Don't forget that verbs in biographies are usually in the past.

    c. Write a draft in your notebook and show it to your teacher. Do all the necessary adjustments.

    d. Write a final version of your biography and, if possible, glue pictures of the invention and the inventor.

6 Present your biography to the class and listen to your classmates' presentation. Which one was the most interesting?

TIPS FOR LIFE

Necessity and inventions

1 Read the proverbial saying above and discuss it with your classmates: do you agree or disagree with it? Why?

2 If you were an inventor, what would you invent?

CHECK YOUR PROGRESS	😃	😐	☹️
Personalities/Inventions			
Simple Past of Irregular Verbs			
Listening			
Speaking			
Reading			
Writing			

Unit 8 WHAT TIME WAS SAYURI'S FLIGHT?

1 Look at the picture, talk to a classmate and answer.

   a. Do you like to travel?

   b. Where did you go on your last vacation?

   c. Which city or country would you like to visit? Why?

2 Read and listen to the dialog. Then act out.

🔊 47

Allan: What did Sayuri do yesterday morning at school?

Kitty: She said goodbye to all students and teachers. Then we threw her a farewell party.

Jim: Then where did she go?

Kitty: She went to the mall and bought some souvenirs to take to her parents, brothers and friends in Japan.

Leo: What kind of souvenirs did she buy?

Carol: She bought T-shirts, caps, and some local arts and crafts… Nothing very expensive, because she didn't have much money.

Kitty: While she was shopping, she met Mr. Jones, the school principal, and thanked him for the hospitality.

Jim: Sayuri's exchange program was a success. She learned a lot from us and we learned a lot from her.

Allan: What time was Sayuri's flight? Who took her to the airport?

Kitty: My parents and I did. Her flight was scheduled to depart at 8 p.m. We helped her with her luggage, and we arrived at the airport in time. But we were very sad. Carol and I were crying when she left.

3 Check the correct information according to the dialog.

   a. ◯ Sayuri bought expensive gifts for her family and friends.

   b. ◯ Sayuri's friends threw her a farewell party.

   c. ◯ She didn't go back to Japan.

   d. ◯ Her flight departed at 8 p.m.

CROSS CULTURAL

Farewell party is an event to say goodbye to someone, especially for those who are traveling abroad.

THINKING AHEAD

1 Read and match the words to their correct definitions.

a. Overweight ◯ A short stay in a place before getting to the final destination.
b. Airline ◯ A card that allows you to board an aircraft.
c. Boarding pass ◯ It allows you to travel in only one direction.
d. One-way ticket ◯ Too heavy.
e. Long flight ◯ A business that carries passengers and/or products by aircraft.
f. Stopover ◯ Traveling a long distance flight.

What's the difference between suitcase and luggage?

Suitcase: large, rectangular container with a handle, for carrying clothes and possessions while traveling.

Luggage: the bags, suitcases, etc. that contain your possessions and that you take with you when you are traveling.

Observe the different way of spelling the verb: Travelling (British English)/Traveling (American English).

Available at: <https://dictionary.cambridge.org/pt/dicionario/ingles/>. Accessed on: Feb. 14, 2019.

A WORD WORK

1 When João Victor and Maria Lucia arrived at the airport, they didn't know many English words. Listen to the words and expressions they had to learn.

gate

plane

weighing machine

conveyor belt/
baggage carousel

metal detector

departure lounge

arrivals and departures board

check-in desk

trolley   luggage

seat belt

customs

2. Find and circle seven words related to traveling in the wordsearch below.

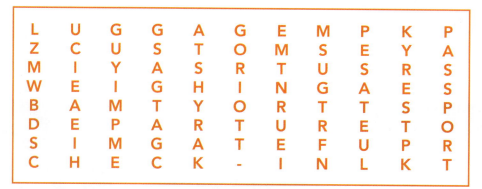

3. Look at the picture and read the text. Then fill in the gaps using the words you found in the wordsearch in activity 2.

Phillip arrived at the airport. While he was walking towards the _____ desk, he looked at the clock and realized he was late.

He reached the check-in desk, put the _____ on the _____ machine and showed his _____ to the clerk.

"_____15A", said the clerk, and Phillip ran to the _____ lounge.

He showed his passport to the _____ officer and said, "I'm very late. Can I board the plane?"

The officer said, "I'm afraid not. Your passport has expired."

"Oh, no!"

Let's play **Can game**, **Mime: Where are you?** and **Clock**.

FOCUS ON LANGUAGE

1 In pairs, read the dialog and check the correct items.

a. The girl is talking about…

   ○ her everyday life.
   ○ her plans for the future.
   ○ actions that happened the day before.

b. When the girl says **I was watching TV**, she's referring to…

   ○ a prediction about her next steps.
   ○ an ongoing action that took place in the past.
   ○ an action that could have happened, but it was avoided.

Go to page 160.

2 Look at the chart. Then circle the correct answers to complete the following statements correctly.

Past Continuous	
Affirmative	I **was watching** TV. / My parents **were sleeping**.
Interrogative	**Were** you **waiting** for him?
Negative	We **weren't waiting** for him.

a. The Past Continuous is composed by the verb to be in the **past/present** followed by a main verb in the **basic/-ing** form.

b. The use of the verb to be **doesn't vary/varies** according to the subject pronoun.

3. Match the columns according to the picture.

In Europe, it is very common to travel by train for long or short distances. These people were enjoying their journey. When the train stopped…

a. The couple in wagon 1… ◯ were exercising.
b. The boys in wagon 2… ◯ was reading a book.
c. The people in wagon 3… ◯ were having lunch.
d. The people in wagon 4… ◯ was taking pictures.
e. The man in wagon 2… ◯ were dancing.
f. The girl in wagon 1… ◯ were watching TV.

4. Read the statement below and do the following activities.

> While she was shopping, she met Mr. Jones, the school principal.

a. Circle the Past Continuous verb tense.
b. Underline the Simple Past verb tense.

5. Read the chart and complete the sentences with **when** or **while**.

	When and While
Past Continuous + Simple Past (or vice-versa)	My mother **arrived** home while I **was taking** a shower.
	When I **came** home, my sister **was playing** video game.
Past Continuous + Past Continuous	I **was watching** TV while my parents **were sleeping**.

a. When we want to indicate that two actions were in progress at the same time, we use _____.

b. When we want to indicate that an action or event was in progress when something happened, we can use _____ or _____.

6 Write **C** (correct) and **I** (incorrect) for the use of **when** and **while**.

a. ◯ My mother hugged me when I was studying.

b. ◯ While Carol knocked on the door, Jim was making cookies.

c. ◯ Susy plays the guitar when I was checking my emails.

d. ◯ We didn't hear anything. I was sleeping while my brother was singing.

7 Read the sentences and write the linking words in the chart, according to the idea they express.

> She said goodbye to all students **and** teachers. **Then** we threw her a farewell party.
>
> She bought T-shirts, caps, and some local arts and crafts... Nothing very expensive, **because** she didn't have much money.
>
> We helped her with her luggage, and we arrived at the airport in time. **But** we were very sad.

Linking Words		
Addition	Add an ideia or information.	also, _____
Contrast/ Opposition	Put together ideas that are different from each other.	however, _____
Cause	Indicate the reason of something.	since, _____
Sequence	Organize the ideas, putting them in order.	next, _____

8 What is a linking word? Check the correct answer based on activity 7.

a. ◯ It's a word that exclusively joins two verbs.

b. ◯ It's a word that joins two sentences or clauses.

c. ◯ It's a word that separates two sentences from one another.

9 Read the sentences and complete them with the appropriate linking words.

a. I like tomatoes in my salad, _____ my husband doesn't.

b. I prefer orange _____ lemon juice. They have vitamin C.

c. I went to the USA, _____ I went to Spain, my final destination.

d. The passengers were hungry _____ their lunch was delayed.

TELLING THE TIME

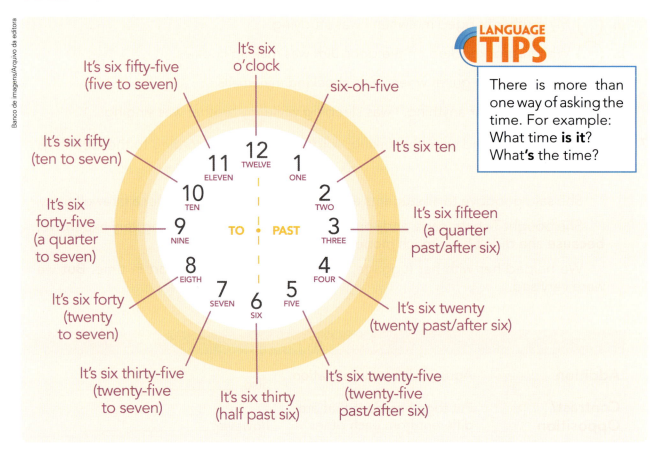

LANGUAGE TIPS

There is more than one way of asking the time. For example: What time **is it**? What**'s** the time?

10 Write the time.

a. 8:00 It's eight _____.

b. 8:05 It's eight-oh-_____.

c. 8:10 _____ ten.

d. 8:35 It's eight _____.

e. 8:40 It's eight _____.

f. 8:45 It's eight _____.

11 There are different time zones around the world. Look and answer: What time is it in...?

a. Germany	b. Hong Kong	c. South Africa	d. Argentina

_____	_____	_____	_____

LISTEN AND SPEAK

1 At the airport, do you know what to do at the check-in desk? Share ideas with your classmates.

2 Listen to the dialog and check the true sentences. Correct the false ones.
🔊 49

a. ◯ The passenger's name is J. Smith.
_____

b. ◯ She is traveling alone.
_____

c. ◯ She wants the aisle sit.
_____

d. ◯ The gate number is 25.
_____

e. ◯ The flight is on time.
_____

3 Miss Roberts is on board the aircraft. She is watching the safety instructions video. Listen
🔊 50 to the procedures recommended and put them in the correct order.

a. ◯ Take a moment to watch the emergency procedure video now.

b. ◯ A life vest is located under your seat. It is reversible and slips over the head.

c. ◯ There is an emergency lighting which is illuminated along the floor leading to all close exits and slides.

d. ◯ Please, fasten your seat belt by inserting the metal tab into the buckle and pull the straps tight.

e. ◯ Please, take a minute to locate the emergency exit closest to your seat.

f. ◯ Good evening, ladies and gentlemen! Welcome to flight 55BA to London. Please pay attention to the emergency procedures. Thanks for flying with us.

ONE HUNDRED AND TWENTY-THREE 123

4 Kitty is talking to a friend about a trip to London with her family. Listen and complete the dialog. Then, in pairs, act it out.

51

Carol: Where _____ you _____ last vacation?

Kitty: We _____ to London.

Carol: And did you _____ the trip?

Kitty: Not at all. It was terrible, in fact!

Carol: Why was it so terrible?

Kitty: Because it was _____ cats and dogs when we _____ there.

Carol: Did anything else _____?

Kitty: Yes! While we were _____ for a restaurant, dad _____ the car.

Carol: What a pity!

5 In pairs, discuss: do emergency procedures videos help save lives? Why (not)?

PRONUNCIATION CORNER

1 Listen and act out the jazz chant.

52

What is her **name**?
Her name is Sibyl.
Where does she **live**?
She lives in Brazil.
What does she **do** in Brazil?
She cooks at Bill's.
What kind of music does she **like**?
She likes samba but Bill likes rock.

Why don't you like **rock**, Sibyl?
Bill likes rock, I like samba.
Where is **Bill**, Sibyl?
He's in bed, he's ill.
How is **Bill**, Sibyl?
He is ill, very ill.
Poor **Sibyl**!
Poor Bill!

2 Listen and practice *Wh-* questions intonation.

53

How can **I help** you? Why is she **cry**ing? Where are you **from**?

3 In pairs, write a short dialog using *Wh-* questions. Then act it out.

_____
_____
_____

READ AND WRITE

1 Discuss the questions below with a classmate.
  a. Do you like to surf the internet?
  b. Which websites do you usually visit?

2 Look at the layout, picture and structure of the following text and answer.
  a. Where was the text extracted from?

  b. What do you know about blogs?

3 What do you expect to read about in the text below?

4 Read the text to check if your prediction in activity 3 was correct. Then discuss the following questions with your classmates and teacher.

www.travelforteens.com/blog/tips-for-a-fun-and-successful-summer-abroad/

Cultural Awareness

[...] Just like the ability to adapt to unexpected changes, it is just as important to be aware of the cultures of the countries that you travel to. This way you won't be totally off guard when people around you at a Chinese restaurant loudly burp after a meal in order to show their satisfaction with the meal or when a South African call you "my bru" (my friend) and invites you to a "braai" (barbecue). When you are open to learning about the culture of a country, you will have friends no matter where your travels take you.

Available at: <www.travelforteens.com/blog/tips-for-a-fun-and-successful-summer-abroad/>.
Accessed on: Feb. 8, 2019.

  a. The text presents two different cultural situations. Which one is the most unusual to you? Why?
  b. Do you agree that adaptability is as important as cultural awareness?
  c. What are the benefits of being open to learn about new cultures?

5 Now it's your turn! Write a comment to the blog post from activity 4, share a cultural awareness experience you had during your last trip. Follow the instructions.

   a. Before writing your comment, answer these questions.
   - Where did you travel to?
   - When did you go?
   - What happened there?
   - What did you learn with this experience?

   b. Write a draft in your notebook.
   c. Check the tone of your writing.
   d. Exchange drafts with a classmate and discuss both comments.
   e. Show the draft to your teacher and make the necessary adjustments.
   f. Write a final version of it in your book.

6 Post your comment in the school blog.

TIPS FOR LIFE

Respect diversity!

1. In pairs, discuss: what does the quote mean?

2. Still in pairs, read the dialog on page 115 and answer: what did Sayuri and her friends learn from each other during her stay in the United States?

I TRAVEL THEREFORE I EMBRACE DIVERSITY.

Mimi Thomas

3. Write and role-play with your classmate a dialog that represents one of the situations in the pictures below.

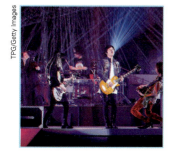  

CHECK YOUR PROGRESS

	😃	😐	🙁
Airport vocabulary			
Past Continuous (When/While)			
Linking words			
Telling the time			
Listening			
Speaking			
Reading			
Writing			

REVIEW
UNITS 7 AND 8

1 Complete the story according to the comic strip. Use the Simple Past or the Past Continuous.

Garfield _____ (do) the newspaper crossword puzzle when a spider _____ (come) into the room. While the spider _____ (climb) up the wall, Garfield _____ (hit) it with the newspaper. Garfield _____ (look) at the wall and _____ (see) a black smudge left by the spider. He thought for a few minutes and… then he _____ (take) his black pencil and _____ (draw) a flower in a pot where the spider was!

2 In pairs, reorder Bob and Vicky's conversation.

○ **Vicky:** Hi, Bob. Did you see Priscilla yesterday?
○ **Bob:** No, I didn't. I should have studied a little bit more!
○ **Bob:** No, I didn't. I saw her last Monday. She traveled with her mother yesterday.
○ **Vicky:** And you, did you go to Los Angeles last Saturday?
○ **Vicky:** Where did she go?
○ **Bob:** She went to San Francisco to stay at her grandfather's house.
○ **Bob:** No, I didn't. I had to study for the final test.
○ **Vicky:** Did you get good grades?

3 Fill in the gaps with **when** or **while**.

a. I was texting my friend _____ I heard a noise at the door.

b. _____ Samuel was eating breakfast quietly, his father left for work.

c. Linda met her husband _____ she was traveling to Italy.

d. John took a selfie _____ Mary was making strange faces.

e. Billy was skateboarding _____ the rain started.

4 Read the sentences and complete with the Simple Past or the Past Continuous.

a. I _____ (eat) a hot dog when my mother _____ me (call).

b. While Tom _____ (go) to school, he _____ (see) Mr. Brown, his Geography teacher, on the street.

c. Debby _____ (play) video game while her sister _____ a shower (take).

d. I _____ (watch) a funny movie on TV when Peter _____ (text) me.

e. Beth _____ (cook) dinner when her father _____ (arrive) home from work.

f. When Paul _____ (get) at the station, the train _____ already _____ (leave).

5 Choose the correct linking words to complete the sentences.

a. I can't speak Japanese, _____ I can speak English.
   ○ but   ○ and   ○ because

b. Melanie can dance _____ sing very well.
   ○ or   ○ after   ○ and

c. Thomas had his eyes closed _____ he was really tired.
   ○ then   ○ because   ○ before

d. He missed the school bus this morning, _____ his father had to drive him.
   ○ then   ○ and   ○ but

EXTRA PRACTICE

UNITS 1 AND 2

1. Read the poster and check the correct answer. What is it about?

DROP YOUR DRAWERS HERE...SOCKS TOO!

Donate packages of new underwear and socks.

Clothes To Kids of Fairfield County provides quality school clothing to low-income or in-crisis school age children in Fairfield County, free of charge.

Included in a full week's worth of school clothes are new underwear and socks. And we need lots of them! All sizes, for boys and girls in grades K-12 (must be in unopened packages, please).

For a complete list of accepted items, visit **clothestokidsfairfieldcounty.org**

Clothes To Kids of Fairfield County
Clothe a Child ~ Change a Life℠

We envision a community in which every school-age child has quality clothing so that he or she may attend school with the confidence and self-esteem needed to achieve academic success.
Clothes To Kids of Fairfield County is a 501 (C)(3) nonprofit organization.

a. ◯ It is about a campaign for clothes donation.
b. ◯ It is about closet and drawers.
c. ◯ It is about socks on sale.

2 Read the poster again and complete the chart with the words and expressions from the box.

> new   school age   underwear and socks
> donation   low income or in-crisis children

Purpose	
Items	
Condition of the items	
Items to be delivered to	
Age	

3 Read the poster once more and correct the statements.

a. Donate new underwear and used socks.
_____

b. Items can be in open packages.
_____

c. Children pay a low fee to receive the items.
_____

d. The items must be small size.
_____

4 Find words in the poster from activity 1 that have the same meaning of the expressions below.

a. underwear _____

b. fall vertically _____

c. to ask an amount of money for something _____

d. an object wrapped in paper or plastic, or packed in a box _____

5 Answer the following questions. Then discuss your answers with a classmate.

a. Do you have siblings? Do you get hand-me-down clothes?
_____

b. Do you use second hand clothes?
_____

c. Do you donate the clothes you don't use anymore?
_____

EXTRA PRACTICE

UNITS 3 AND 4

1 Read the blog post and check the correct answer. What is it about?

www.metmuseum.org/blogs/teen-blog

BLOGS/TEEN BLOG

What's up with the No Touching Rule?
September 13, 2016
Stephanie M., Former High School Intern

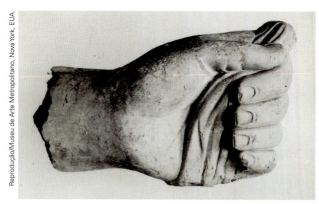

Hand. 3rd-7th century. Central Asia. Red clay; 8in. × 4 1/2in. (20.3cm × 11.4cm). The Metropolitan Museum of Art, New York, Rogers Fund. 1930

As a child, I frequently visited The Met to observe all the different aspects of art. That's right — observe or look only with my eyes. This may seem silly, but to a young child observing is like the next *Mission Impossible*. Don't get me wrong; I loved coming to the museum (I still do!), but I just thought it was so unfair that I couldn't feel the beauty of the art with my fingers. I was always taught that "sharing is caring," and to me, neither the artist nor the Museum staff were being caring enough to let me put my finger on anything. Was the artist just being greedy by not wanting anyone to touch what he made? As I grew up, and especially while interning at The Met this summer, I came to understand the true purpose of this rule.

I now see that at a place like The Met, with all its valuable treasures, this rule is not meant to deter people from the art, but rather to preserve its longevity […] Through the "no touching" rule, I learned that art does not need to be touched in order for it to be felt. […] This intangible connection is formed (most often) without touch.

Available at: <https://www.metmuseum.org/blogs/teen-blog/2016/no-touching>. Accessed on: Mar. 7, 2019.

a. ◯ It is about teens visit to the museum.
b. ◯ It is about museum rules.
c. ◯ It is about a high school intern.

2 Read the blog post again and match the questions to the correct answers.

a. When was the post made?
b. Who is Stephanie M.?
c. What was her opinion about observing the art in the museum?
d. What does she compare the act of observing with?
e. Does she understand the "no touching" rule now?
f. Stephanie understood that…

○ She thinks it was like the next *Mission Impossible*.
○ She is a former high school intern at the museum.
○ museum rules are there to preserve art longevity.
○ She thought it was unfair that she was not allowed to touch it.
○ Yes, she does.
○ September 13, 2016.

3 Read the blog post once more and answer T (true) or F (false).

a. ○ She talks about her visits to the museum as a child.
b. ○ To a young child, observing is easy.
c. ○ She loves going to the museum.
d. ○ She can't touch the art with her fingers.
e. ○ She thinks the museum staff is not caring.

4 The following words were extracted from the text. Read them and complete the gaps with a synonym from the box.

| look at | old | ridiculous |
| feel | wrongful | repeatedly |

a. former _____
b. frequently _____
c. observe _____
d. silly _____
e. unfair _____
f. touch _____

5 Do some research on rules that have to be followed when you are in a museum and share the results with your classmates.

EXTRA PRACTICE

UNITS 5 AND 6

1 Read the text below and check the picture that best suits its main idea.

> https://easyscienceforkids.com/understanding-the-weather-forecast/
>
> ### Understanding the Weather Forecast
>
> "A low pressure system is moving into our area tonight." "The relative humidity level is at 30 percent." "Winds are moving out of the northwest at 20 miles per hour." You might have heard a weather forecaster make comments like these, but do you know what they mean?
>
> Weather forecasters rely on computer data, satellite images and their own observations to accurately forecast the weather. They've also got their own language for explaining it. Read on to learn how to understand a weather forecast. [...]
>
> - A high pressure system occurs when dry, cool air spirals in a clockwise direction, bringing mild weather and sunny, blue skies.
> - A low pressure system is moist, warm air swirling in a counter-clockwise direction. Low pressure systems usually mean stormy, wet weather.
> - Relative humidity refers to how much moisture is in the air compared with how much moisture the air can hold. The more humid it is, the warmer you feel in hot weather and the colder you feel in winter weather.
> - A front is when two air masses of different temperatures meet. When cold and warm air masses meet, you can usually expect turbulent, stormy weather.
> - A cold front happens when cold air and bad weather moves into an area. [...] A warm front occurs when warm air moves into an area. [...]
>
>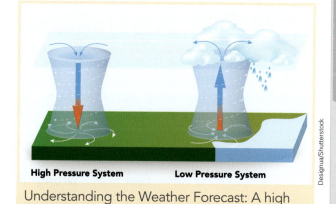
>
> Understanding the Weather Forecast: A high pressure system bringing mild weather and sunny, blue skies. Low pressure systems usually mean stormy, wet weather.

Available at: <https://easyscienceforkids.com/understanding-the-weather-forecast/>. Accessed on: Mar. 10, 2019.

a.

b.

c.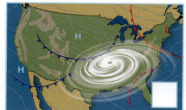

2 Match the words to their correct meaning, according to the text.

a. turbulent ◯ information and statistics
b. observations ◯ wet
c. data ◯ rough
d. forecaster ◯ a weather reporter
e. moist ◯ method that consists on understanding something through watching and studying

3 Read the sentences and circle the words that complete them correctly.

a. Weather forecasters **don't use/use** satellite data.
b. There are specific **words/numbers** used by weather forecasters.
c. A **high/low** pressure system brings sunny weather and clear skies.
d. If it is humid, it means you feel **colder/warmer** in winter.
e. When two air masses of different temperatures meet, we can expect **sunny weather/stormy weather**.

4 Read the article one more time and check **right**, **wrong** or **not mentioned**.

a. Computer data is not used to forecast the weather.
  ◯ Right   ◯ Wrong   ◯ Not mentioned

b. Most tornadoes form from thunderstorms.
  ◯ Right   ◯ Wrong   ◯ Not mentioned

c. Stormy weather happens during low pressure systems.
  ◯ Right   ◯ Wrong   ◯ Not mentioned

d. A cold front happens when cold air and bad weather moves into an area.
  ◯ Right   ◯ Wrong   ◯ Not mentioned

5 What is the weather forecast for tomorrow in the city you live in?

Weather forecast for tomorrow: _____/_____/_____ at 7:00 a.m.

a. Low temperature: _____

b. High temperature: _____

c. Humidity: _____

EXTRA PRACTICE

UNITS 7 AND 8

1 Read the text and check the correct answer. The text is…

a. ◯ an article.   b. ◯ a timeline.   c. ◯ a biography.

EVOLUTION OF THE ALARM CLOCK

One of the first forms of the modern alarm clock was drinking excessive amounts of water prior to sleeping.

During ancient times people also utilized the sun as a method of getting out of bed in the morning.

Knocker-ups were hired from the 18th until the 20th century to knock on a client's window with a stick to wake them up.

Factory whistles were used during the Industrial Revolution to release a shrill sound to awaken the company's worker.

Bell Towers were extremely large, mechanical, analog clocks that were set to sound the bells at a specific time every day.

It wasn't until 1876 that Seth Thomas invented a mechanical clock attached with an alarm mechanism that was eventually mass produced through his company Seth E. Thomas Clock Company.

During the 1940's the invention of the radio alarm clock emerged.

The snooze button was first introduced by General Electric-Telechron when they released the Snooze-Alarm.

In today's society people most commonly use their smartphones as their preferred alarm clock.

2 Number the events regarding the evolution of the alarm clock, according to the text.

- ◯ the sound of bell towers
- ◯ drinking water
- ◯ mechanical clock
- ◯ snooze button
- ◯ someone knocking at a client's window
- ◯ radio alarm clock
- ◯ the sound of factory whistles
- ◯ smartphones used as alarm clocks
- ◯ observing the sun

3 Read the text again and answer **T** (true) or **F** (false).

a. ◯ People use their smartphones only to make calls.

b. ◯ The radio alarm clock was invented in 1876.

c. ◯ Drinking lots of water before going to bed helped people wake up early.

d. ◯ A long time ago people were hired to knock on someone's window as a form of alarm clock.

e. ◯ The moon was used as a way to wake up people.

4 Match the words from the box to their definitions.

> factory   analog
> knock   snooze   ancient

a. To have a short sleep. _____

b. A type of mechanical clock. _____

c. A building or group of buildings where products are made. _____

d. The same as "old". _____

e. To hit or strike a surface noisily to attract attention. _____

5 How do you know when it is time to wake up? Discuss with your classmates and teacher.

PROJECT 1
MAKING ART

1 Look at the artwork painted by Mexican street artist Farid Rueda and answer the questions. Then discuss them with your classmates and teacher.

a. What can you see in this artwork? Which elements call your attention? How do you feel when you look at it?

b. Do you think that making art is a way to express emotions? Why (not)?

c. In your opinion, does this artwork express emotions? Explain your answer.

2. In pairs, read the text about creating art to balance emotions. Then answer the questions.

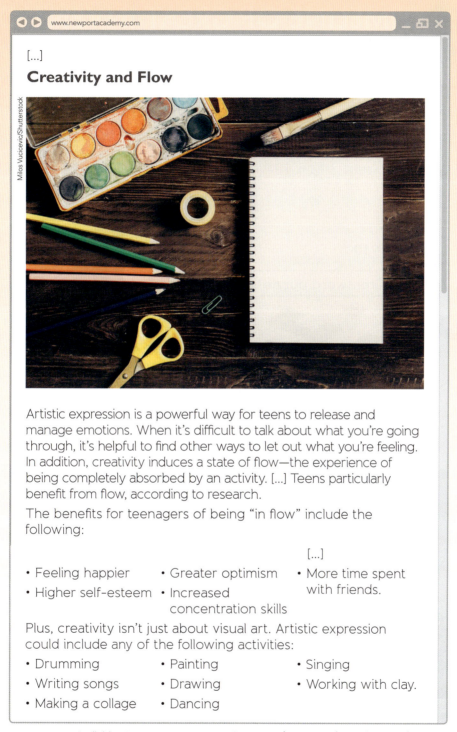

[...]
Creativity and Flow

Artistic expression is a powerful way for teens to release and manage emotions. When it's difficult to talk about what you're going through, it's helpful to find other ways to let out what you're feeling. In addition, creativity induces a state of flow—the experience of being completely absorbed by an activity. [...] Teens particularly benefit from flow, according to research.

The benefits for teenagers of being "in flow" include the following:

[...]

- Feeling happier
- Higher self-esteem
- Greater optimism
- Increased concentration skills
- More time spent with friends.

Plus, creativity isn't just about visual art. Artistic expression could include any of the following activities:

- Drumming
- Writing songs
- Making a collage
- Painting
- Drawing
- Dancing
- Singing
- Working with clay.

Available at: <www.newportacademy.com/resources/mental-health/5-ways-balance-teen-emotions-well-being/>. Accessed on: Mar. 8, 2019.

a. Do you agree that making art is a way to release and manage emotions? Why (not)?

b. Do you feel any of the previously mentioned benefits when you create art? Which one?

3. It's time for you to express yourself through art. Create an artwork to exhibit at an art festival that will take place in your school.

PROJECT 2
TIMELINE OF GREAT INVENTIONS

1 Look at the timeline and answer the questions.

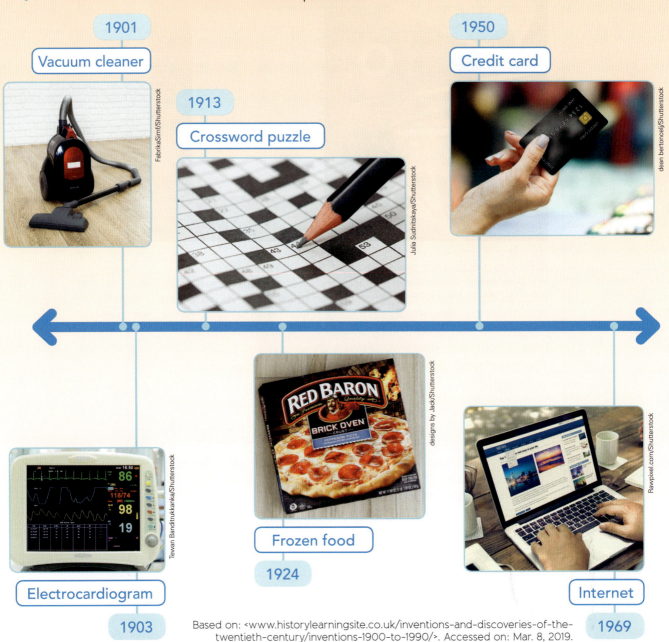

Based on: <www.historylearningsite.co.uk/inventions-and-discoveries-of-the-twentieth-century/inventions-1900-to-1990/>. Accessed on: Mar. 8, 2019.

a. Which of the inventions above do you consider more useful to society in general? Why?

b. Do any of the timeline inventions influence your life? Explain your answer.

c. Choose one of the inventions above and make a short description of it.

2. Read the text about an important invention made by Hannah Herbst. Then answer the questions.

Hannah Herbst, 17, Florida

Herbst was inspired to invent at the age of 15 by her then-nine-year-old pen pal, who lives in Ethiopia and did not have access to lights. This is surprisingly common: there are 1.3 billion people alive today without electricity. So this student came up with the Beacon (Bringing Electricity Access to Countries through Ocean Energy), which captures energy directly from ocean waves.

The Beacon can create electricity from almost any water source.

Herbst's thinking was that populations tend to settle around bodies of water; about 40% of the world's population lives within 100km (62 miles) of the coast and only 10% lives further than 10km (6.2 miles) away from a source of freshwater that you don't have to dig for, such as a river or lake.

The technology consists of a hollow plastic tube, with a propeller at one end and a hydroelectric generator at the other. As tidal energy drives the propeller, it's converted into useable energy by the generator. After designing a prototype turbine as a computer model, Herbst 3D-printed a prototype which she tested in an intercoastal waterway.

If the design were to be scaled up, Herbst has calculated that Beacon could charge three car batteries simultaneously in an hour. She suggests that the energy generated could be used to power water purification technologies, or blood centrifuges at hospitals in the developing world.

The invention won the Discovery Education 3M Young Scientist Challenge in 2015, among numerous other awards, and Herbst is currently studying for a degree in computer engineering while she completes high school. [...]

Available at: <www.bbc.com/future/story/20180316-four-teenage-inventors-changing-the-world>.
Accessed on: Mar. 8, 2019.

a. Skim the text and look up in the dictionary the meaning of the words you don't know.

b. In your opinion, was Herbst's invention important to society? Why (not)?

c. Think about the problems that happen in the world or in your community. Can you create an important invention that could solve them? Explain your answer.

3. Now it's your time to create an invention. Follow the instructions your teacher is going to give you and get to work.

FUN ACTIVITIES 1

1 What are these people doing? Match the pictures to the sentences.

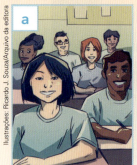

○ People from all around the world are practicing English and making new friends at a gathering.

○ Azad is planning a trip to Ireland to continue his studies.

○ Mark and Susan are living in China to learn more about Chinese culture.

○ Kyoko is having English classes as part of an exchange program.

○ Jimena is saying goodbye to her family because she is going to study abroad.

2 Circle the pictures that represent sustainable actions.

a.

Carla buys clothes at a second-hand store.

b.

Michael has too many pieces of clothes.

c.

Bradley usually separates clothes for donation.

d.

Sandra goes shopping at a charity bazaar.

3 Unscramble the letters of the words in parentheses to complete the sentences and find out what Julie usually eats every day.

Hello! I'm Julie and I like to eat healthy food. Breakfast is my favorite _____ (elam) of the day, so I have scrambled _____ (sgeg), two whole wheat _____ (tastos), orange _____ (ieujc) and fresh _____ (fritu). For lunch, I usually eat a _____ (aadsl), some cooked _____ (legsetavbe) and a veggie _____ (iep) or an _____ (lomeeett). For a snack, I drink _____ (ate) and eat three toasts with white _____ (eheces). For dinner, I usually eat cooked vegetables with _____ (qouian).

4 Look at the pictures and complete the crossword with the name of these art expressions.

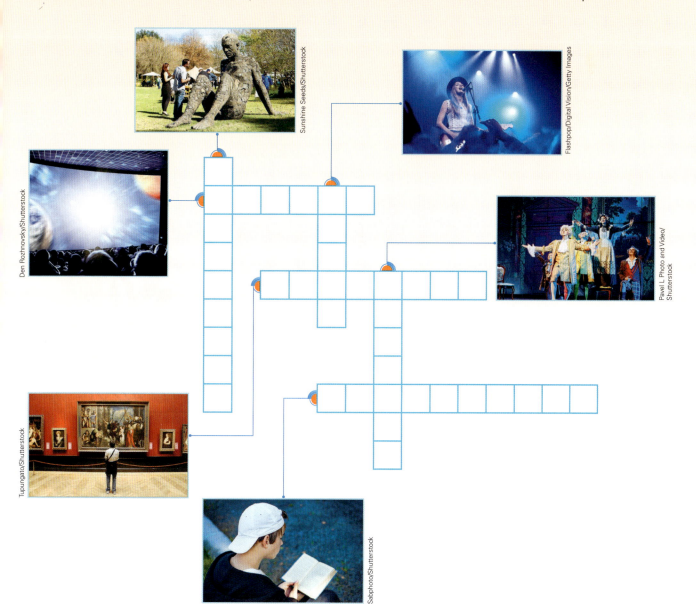

FUN ACTIVITIES 2

1 Fill in the blanks with the words from the box to complete this week's weather forecast. You can use the same word more than once.

rainy   sunny   cloudy

	Sunday	Monday	Tuesday	Wednesday	Thursday	Friday	Saturday
Forecast	☀	☀	☁	☁	☀	☁	🌧
Temperature (average)	17°	19°	16°	16°	19°	17°	18°

2 Break the code and find out why Alex is so happy.

_____
_____

3 Find and circle in the wordsearch the name of the inventions.

```
A I R P L A N E E V T R
U O C O N P O T X R C N
T E J Q D T R E C V A V
O R D F D U K L N Q M B
M C O M P U T E R A E O
O N H D P O V L G T R M
B C F O A I R I S H A X
I H H P N U I S S V H J
L X A A M E A I J U U W
E E S D Q X N O Q S A P
N B X C C F G N G V J W
U P T E L E P H O N E X
```

4 What does Brenda do in the morning? Look at the four clocks and write the correct time in the gaps.

It's _____ a.m.

It's _____ a.m.

It's _____ a.m.

It's _____ a.m.

GLOSSARY

a few: alguns/algumas
a little: um pouco
abroad: no exterior, em outro país
absent: ausente
acclaim: aclamar
actress: atriz
actually: na verdade; na realidade
adaptability: adaptabilidade; flexibilidade
add: adicionar, acrescentar
adjustment: ajuste
advice: conselho
adviser: orientador/a
aircraft: avião, aeronave
airplane: avião
aisle: corredor
allowance: mesada
almost: quase
alone: sozinho/a
although: embora, apesar de
anniversary: aniversário (de acontecimento)
anybody: alguém; qualquer um/a
anyone: alguém; qualquer um/a
anything: qualquer coisa
appetizer: entrada, antepasto
apple: maçã
application form: formulário
approach: abordar; abordagem
arrival: chegada; desembarque
arrive: chegar
artwork: obra de arte
as long as: tanto quanto
assembly line: linha de montagem
assure: garantir
attach: anexar
attachment: anexo/a
attend: ir a, frequentar
available: disponível
award: prêmio
awareness: consciência; conscientização
awesome: impressionante, legal

babysitter: babá
bagel: pão em forma de rosca
bake: assar
baking powder: fermento em pó
balloon: balão, bexiga
barbecue: churrasco
bathroom: banheiro
batter: batedor/a
batting: rebatendo com bastão
battlefield: campo de batalha
be born: nascer
beautiful: bonito/a
become: tornar-se
bedtime: hora de dormir
begin: começar, iniciar
belong: pertencer
besides: além de
bet: aposta; apostar
bin: caixa, lata, cesto
binder: fichário
birth: nascimento
black: preto/a
blazer: paletó
blend: misturar
blind: cego
blood: sangue
blouse: blusa
boarding pass: cartão de embarque
bold: arrojado/a
book: livro; fazer reserva
bookworm: "rato" de biblioteca
booth: cabine, barraca
bracelet: pulseira
brackets: parênteses
bran: farelo
brand: marca
break: pausar; quebrar
breakfast: café da manhã
brief: breve
broke: quebrou
broth: caldo
brown: marrom
brunch: misto de café da manhã e almoço
buckle: fivela
bully: intimidar, ameaçar
burp: arrotar
business-woman: mulher de negócios

busy: ocupado/a
butter: manteiga
button: botão

cake: bolo
candy: doce, chocolate
cane: bengala
cap: boné
capable: capaz
care: cuidar; cuidado
career: carreira
careful: cuidadoso/a
carry: carregar
cashier: caixa (funcionário/a) de loja, de banco, etc.
catch: apanhar
catchy: marcante
cater: serviço de bufê
cent: centavo
chalk: giz
check: verificar, marcar
check-in desk: balcão de check-in
chicken breast: peito de frango
childhood: infância
chilly: gelado/a; frio/a
chimney: chaminé
clap: aplaudir, bater palmas
crouton: cubinho de pão torrado
chase: perseguir
clash: choque
clear: claro/a, transparente
clearly: claramente
closely: próximo/a
closet: armário
cloth: tecido, pano
cloud: nuvem
cloudy: nublado/a
clue: indício, pista
concert hall: sala de concerto
co-worker: colega de trabalho
cock: galo
cookbook: livro de receitas
collector: colecionador/a; cobrador/a de impostos
color: cor; colorir
comic strip: tira de quadrinhos
comic book: revista em quadrinhos, gibi

commitment: compromisso
complaining: reclamação
countable: contável
composition: redação
crossword puzzle: palavras cruzadas
conductor: motorista; maestro/maestrina
chair: cadeira
coffee: café
consumer: consumidor
contain: conter
contest: concurso
content: conteúdo
cocoa: cacau
corn: milho
clothes: roupas
cost: custar
cough: tossir; tosse
couple: par, casal
course: curso
cover: capa
crayon: giz de cera
crop: colheita, safra
conveyor belt: esteira
customs: alfândega
converter: conversor
couple: algum/a; casal
coldness: frieza
cottage cheese: queijo fresco
clerk: atendente
chamber piece: música de câmara
convey: transmitir, expressar
cup: xícara
come up: surgir
claim: alegar, afirmar
craft: artesanato
cry: chorar
charge: cobrar
crash: bater

damage: danificar
daughter: filha
day-by-day: dia a dia; diário/a
death: morte
death toll: número de mortos
decay: deterioração
deeply: profundamente
degree: grau

146 **ONE HUNDRED AND FORTY-SIX**

delayed: atrasado/a
delivery: entrega
denser: mais denso
departure: partida; embarque
depict: retratar, representar
derive: derivar
desk: mesa de escritório, carteira escolar
dessert: sobremesa
detail: detalhe
dietician: dietista, nutricionista
difficult: difícil
dinner: jantar
directly: diretamente
dirigible: dirigível
dirty: sujo/a
disagree: discordar
disagreement: discordância
display: monitor
doctor: tratar, medicar; médico/a; doutor/a
donate: doar
done: feito
donkey: asno, burro
dot: ponto
doubt: dúvida
downtown: centro da cidade
drawer: gaveta
drawing: desenho
dress: vestido
dressing: tempero (de salada)
dripping: pingando
drown: afogar (-se)
drums: bateria
dry: seco/a
due: devido a
dwarf: anão/anã

ear: orelha
earned: ganho
earring: brinco
easier: mais fácil
easy: fácil
elderly: idoso/a
electric guitar: guitarra
elementary: básico/a
empowerment: conferir poder a, empoderar
enable: possibilitar
ending: final
endless: interminável
enough: suficiente
even: quite
every day: todos os dias
everywhere: em todo lugar, em toda parte
exchange: troca; intercâmbio (estudantil)
exercise: fazer exercícios
exhibition: exposição
exit: saída
expected: esperado/a

expert: especialista
expired: expirou
expose: expor
eye: olho

facade: fachada
face: enfrentar
fairy: fada
fall: outono
farewell: despedida; adeus
fashion: moda
fasten: fechar; afivelar
faucet: torneira
feel: sentir
fever: febre
few: poucos/as
fifth: quinto/a
fighter: avião de caça
file: arquivo
fill: preencher
find: achar, encontrar; descobrir
find out: descobrir
fireplace: lareira
fit: caber; estar em forma
fix: consertar
flat: plano
flavor: sabor
flight: voo
flip-flop: chinelo de dedo
float: boia
flood: inundação
floor: piso; andar
flour: farinha
flower: flor
flu: gripe
fly: voar
flyer: folheto
foggy: neblina, névoa
foreign: estrangeiro/a, de fora
form: formulário
forum: reunião
frame: moldura
freely: livremente
free-standing: independente
freeze: congelar
French fries: batatas fritas
French toast: rabanada
Friday: sexta-feira
frighten: assustar

gadget: equipamento
garment: peça de roupa
gate: portão
get up: levantar
giant: gigante
glass: copo
go hiking: fazer caminhada
goggles: óculos de natação
grade: nota; série, classe

grandma: vovó
grandpa: vovô
grant: conceder
gray: cinza
greasy: gorduroso/a
great grandparents: bisavós
greed: ganância
green: verde
greet: cumprimentar
grilled: grelhado/a
guest: convidado/a
gulf: golfo

hailing: saudar, elogiar, chover granizo
ham: presunto
hand: mão
handheld: portátil
handle: lidar; alça
handy: em mãos; útil
hangman: jogo da forca
hard: muito difícil
harvest: colheita
head: cabeça
headline: manchete
headphones: fones de ouvido
healthier: mais saudável
heartbeat: batimento cardíaco
heat: aquecer
helmet: capacete
helpless: indefeso/a
herbal: de ervas
here you are: aqui está você
heritage: patrimônio
herself: ela mesma
high school: ensino médio
hire: contratar
homemade: feito/a em casa
homestay: hospedagem em casa de família
hometown: cidade natal
homework: lição de casa
hope: esperar; esperança
horse: cavalo
horseback riding: andar a cavalo; cavalgar
host: anfitrião/ã; abrigar
hotness: calor
however: no entanto
hungry: com fome
hurry: pressa; apressar-se
hurt: doer, machucar, magoar
husband: marido

ice: gelo
ice cream: sorvete
illnesses: doenças

inexpensive: barato/a
insert: inserir
instant: instantâneo/a
interact: interagir
interview: entrevista
issue: assunto, questão
It's raining cats and dogs: está chovendo muito, está chovendo canivetes

jail: prisão
jewel: pedra preciosa, joia
job: trabalho
jog: praticar corrida
joints: articulações
jouney: viagem

keyboard: teclado
kitchen: cozinha
knock: bater
known: conhecido/a

landfill: lixão, aterro sanitário
large: grande
latest: o último/a, o/a mais recente
laughing: rindo
law: lei
law office: escritório de advocacia
lead: pista; conduzir
leaflet: panfleto
leaves: folhas
leftover: sobras
legacy: legado
lemon: limão-siciliano
lend: emprestar
less: menos
level: nível
library: biblioteca
lie: mentir; mentira
lifestyle: estilo de vida
light bulb: lâmpada
lighter: mais leve
lime: limão
lining: forro
linking: ligando
liver: fígado
loaded: carregado/a
look closely: olhar os detalhes
lose: perder
lots of: muitos/as
loud: alto/a
louder: mais alto
lounge: sala
lovely: encantador/a
lower: mais baixo/a
luggage: bagagem

lunch: almoço
lunchtime: hora do almoço
lungs: pulmões

made: feito/a
magazine: revista
main course: prato principal
manager: gerente, administrador/a
maple syrup: xarope de bordo
marketplace: mercado
marry: casar-se
mashed potatoes: purê de batatas
masterpiece: obra-prima
match: relacionar; partida (de jogo)
mate: colega
matter: problema, assunto
meaning: significado
meaningful: significativo
measure: medida
meat: carne
meatball: almôndega
medicine: medicamento
menu: cardápio
might: poder
mild: ameno/a
milk: leite
miller: moleiro
mind: importar-se
miner: mineiro
mirror: espelho
missing: faltando, perdendo
mix: mexer, misturar
moisture: umidade
Monday: segunda-feira
monthly: mensalmente
morning: manhã
mouse: rato
mudslide: deslizamento de terra
muffin: bolinho
mug: caneca
musician: músico, musicista
mutation: mutação

nearly: aproximadamente
neighbor: vizinho/a
neighborhood: vizinhança
never: nunca
new: novo
newspaper: jornal
night: noite
noise: barulho
noon: meio-dia
northern: do norte
northwest: noroeste
notebook: caderno

notable: notável
not at all: nem um pouco
noun: substantivo
novel: romance

of course: claro
off guard: desavisado/a; desprevenido/a
off-puting: desmotivador/a
old: velho/a
on sale: em liquidação
on the other hand: por outro lado
one-way-ticket: passagem de ida
onion: cebola
orange: laranja
order: ordem; pedido
other: outro/a
otherwise: por outro lado
outfit: roupa
over: acima, além
overweight: excesso de peso

pain: dor
paint: tinta; pintar
painter: pintor/a
painting: pintura
parents: pais
partner: parceiro/a; sócio/a
party: festa
peaceful: pacífico/a
peasant: camponês/a
peck of: grande número ou quantidade de algo
people: pessoas
per: por
pick: pegar
pickle: picles
pickled: em conserva
pie: torta
plain: sem sabor
player: jogador/a
plenty (of): de sobra
poetry: poesia
polluting: poluente
poor: pobre
portrait: retrato
portray: retratar
post: postagem
prediction: previsão
presentation: apresentação
prevent: prevenir
preventable: evitável
price: preço
principal: diretor/a
print: imprimir
printer: impressora
private: particular, privado/a
prize: prêmio

procedure: procedimento
proceed: continuar; ir em frente
processor: processador
promise: prometer
publish: publicar
purpose: propósito, intenção
purse: bolsa
push away: empurrar

question: pergunta
quickly: rapidamente
quiet: quieto/a; calmo/a

rabbit: coelho
race: corrida
railway: estrada de ferro
rain: chuva
rainy: chuvoso
raise: levantar, erguer
rare: raro/a
rat: rato
reach: alcançar, atingir
really: realmente, de verdade
reason: razão
receive: receber
recognize: reconhecer
record: registro; gravar
red: vermelho/a
redeeming: redimir; salvar
regarded: reconhecido/a
regular: comum
relationship: relacionamento
reliable: confiável
remember: lembrar
reminded: lembrado/a
reopening: reabertura
repertoire: repertório
report: relatar; previsão, relatório
rescue: resgate; resgatar
research: pesquisa
rest: descansar; descanso
retire: aposentar
reuse: reutilizar
reveal: revelar
reversible: reversível
rice: arroz
ride up: subir
right now: agora mesmo
ripen: amadurecer
role-play: dramatização
room: cômodo, quarto
rope: corda
round: redondo/a
rubber: borracha
rubbish: lixo
running: corrida

safe: seguro/a
sailing: velejando
salesperson: vendedor/a
sandcastle: castelo de areia
sanitation: saneamento
Saturday: sábado
sausage: salsicha, linguiça
save: salvar; economizar
scale: balança
scaring: assustador/a
scene: cena; cenário
schedule: horário; programa
scissors: tesoura
scrambled: embaralhado/a; mexido/a
screener: analista
seafood: frutos do mar
season: estação
seat: assento
seat belt: cinto de segurança
second-hand: segunda mão
seem: parecer
sergeant: sargento/a
share: compartilhar
sheet: folha de papel
shell: concha, casca
shift: mudança
shine: brilhar
ship: navio
shipping industry: indústria naval
shirt: camisa
shorthand: taquigrafia
shower: ducha; tomar banho
sick: doente
side: lado
simpler: mais simples
singer: cantor/a
single: único/a
sinking: afundando
size: tamanho
skateboarding: andar de skate
ski: esquiar
skirt: saia
sky: céu
slip: escorregar
slumber party: festa do pijama
small: pequeno/a
smart: esperto/a, inteligente
smoked: defumado/a
smudge: mancha
snack: lanche
sneaker: tênis
snowy: coberto de neve
soap opera: novela
soccer: futebol

sock: meia
someone: alguém
sometimes: às vezes
somewhere: em algum lugar
son: filho
songwriter: compositor/a
sore throat: dor de garganta
soul: alma
sound: som; soar
soup: sopa
source: fonte
southern: meridional; do sul
souvenir: lembrança; suvenir
spare time: tempo livre
sparkling: com gás
speech: discurso
speed: velocidade
speed up: acelerar
spider: aranha
spinning wheel: roda de fiar
spread: espalhar
spring: primavera
stand up comedy: espetáculo de humor executado por apenas um comediante, que se apresenta geralmente em pé
starch: amido
starfish: estrela-do-mar
state: estado
statement: afirmação, declaração
stationary: parado/a
steak: bife
steel: aço
step: passo
step-by-step: passo a passo
stir: mexer, misturar
stockings: meia-calça
stomachache: dor de estômago
stopover: escala
store: guardar, armazenar; loja
storm: tempestade
strange: estranho/a
strap: alça, correia
strawberry: morango
stream: riacho, leito
street: rua
stretch: estirar, esticar
striking: notável
stuff: coisa
stuffed: recheado/a
stumble: tropeçar, dar um passo em falso
stunning: maravilhoso/a
subject: sujeito; disciplina
subway: metrô
sugar: açúcar
suit: terno; adequar

suitable: tenho; adequar
suit case: mala
sum up: resumir
Sunday: domingo
sunglasses: óculos de sol
sunny: ensolarado/a
supply: provisão
support: apoiar
surface: superfície
surfer: surfista
sustainable: sustentável
swap: trocar
swear: jurar
sweat: suar
sweater: suéter
sweetheart: querido/a

tab: aba
table tennis: pingue-pongue, tênis de mesa
tablespoon: colher de sopa
take over: assumir
taste: provar; sabor
tax: imposto, taxa
tea: chá
teach: ensinar
teaspoon: colher de chá
teller: caixa de banco (funcionário/a)
terrific: ótimo/a, estupendo/a
test: prova
testimonial: testemunho
thank: agradecer
that: aquele/a
the: o(s), a(s)
the most: o/a mais
the movies: cinema
the wettest: o/a mais molhado/a
thirsty: com sede
thirty: trinta
though: apesar de tudo
thought: pensamento
threat: ameaça
throat: garganta
through: através de; por meio de
throughout: por todo/a
thunder: trovão
Thursday: quinta-feira
tidy up: arrumar, organizar
tie: gravata
tight: apertado, justo
time zone: fuso horário
timeline: linha do tempo
tiny: muito pequeno/a
tired: cansado/a
toll: pedágio
tomorrow: amanhã
tonne: tonelada
toothpick: palito de dentes
toss: jogar; mexer

touch: toque; tocar
towards: em direção a
tracking: rastreamento
travel agent: agente de viagem
traveler: viajante
treat: tratar
trek: caminhar
trigger: gatilho
trimmer: aparador
trip: viagem
trolley: carrinho
trouble: problema
truly: realmente, verdadeiramente
T-shirt: camiseta
Tuesday: terça-feira
tuna: atum
turkey: peru
turn: vez; virar
turn off: desligar
twins: gêmeos/as
twister: furacão, tornado

uncommon: raro/a
uncountable: incontável
understandable: compreensível
undies: roupa de baixo
unhealthy: não saudável
unveiled: exposto/a
unwanted: indesejado/a
unwrap: desembrulhar
upset: abalado/a; chateado/a
use: usar
user: usuário/a
update: atualizado/a

venue: local para eventos e espetáculos
vest: colete
view: visão
viewpoint: ponto de vista
vintage clothes: roupas antigas

wagon: vagão
waitress: garçonete
wake up: acordar
war: guerra
warm: quente
warning: aviso, advertência
wash: lavar
waste: desperdiçar; desperdício
wastebasket: cesto de lixo
watch: assistir; relógio

water: água
way: jeito; caminho
wealth: riqueza, fartura
wear: vestir
weather: tempo
Wednesday: quarta-feira
weekend: fim de semana
weigh: pesar; peso
what: o que
What a pity!: que pena!
What's up?: O que há?; O que está acontecendo?
whatever: seja o que for
wheat: trigo
when: quando
where: onde
whether: se
which: qual, quais
while: enquanto, embora
whistling: assobiando
white: branco/a
who: quem
whom: quem, a quem, que
why: por que (em perguntas)
wife: esposa
willingly: com boa vontade, de bom grado
win: ganhar
wind: vento
windy: de vento, ventania
winner: ganhador/a;
winter: inverno
with: com
without: sem
wizard: mago, feiticeiro/a
wordsearch: caça-palavras
work: trabalho; trabalhar
worker: trabalhador/a
world-class: de classe mundial, renomado
worldwide: mundial, mundialmente
worry: preocupar-se
worship: adorar, cultuar
wrap: embrulhar
writer: escritor/a
written: escrito/a

yankee: pessoa do norte dos Estados Unidos
yellow: amarelo/a
yesterday: ontem
yet: ainda
yourself: você mesmo/a

zip code: código postal

IRREGULAR VERBS

Os verbos podem assumir sentidos diferentes dos listados abaixo, portanto é preciso atentar ao contexto para compreender o significado e o uso de cada um deles.

Base Form	Simple Past	Past Participle	Translation
be	was/were	been	ser; estar
become	became	become	tornar-se
begin	began	begun	começar
buy	bought	bought	comprar
catch	caught	caught	pegar; agarrar
choose	chose	chosen	escolher
come	came	come	vir; chegar
do	did	done	fazer
drink	drank	drunk	beber
drive	drove	driven	dirigir
eat	ate	eaten	comer
fly	flew	flown	voar; pilotar
forget	forgot	forgotten	esquecer
get	got	got/gotten	obter; conseguir; pegar
give	gave	given	dar
go	went	gone	ir
have	had	had	ter
hear	heard	heard	ouvir
know	knew	known	saber; conhecer
let	let	let	deixar; permitir
make	made	made	fazer
say	said	said	dizer
see	saw	seen	ver
send	sent	sent	mandar; enviar
sing	sang	sung	cantar
sleep	slept	slept	dormir
speak	spoke	spoken	falar
swim	swam	swum	nadar
take	took	taken	tomar; pegar; levar
think	thought	thought	pensar
throw	threw	thrown	jogar
wear	wore	worn	usar; vestir
win	won	won	vencer; ganhar
write	wrote	written	escrever

GRAMMAR HELPER

UNIT 1

Present Continuous (-*ing* verbs) – spelling rules

Usamos o **Present Continuous** para descrever ações que estão acontecendo no momento da fala. Observe a regra da terminação -*ing* a seguir.

> **1.** Verbos em geral: acrescenta-se **-ing** ao final da palavra.
>
> **study** – She is study**ing** a new language.
>
> **2.** Verbos terminados em **e**: elimina-se o **e** e acrescenta-se **-ing**:
>
> **practice** – The athlete is practic**ing** for the Olympic games.
>
> **3.** Verbos monossilábicos ou com a última sílaba tônica, terminados em consoante-vogal-consoante: dobra-se a última consoante e acrescenta-se **-ing**:
>
> **begin** – They are begin**ning** their studies.

1 Write the verbs below in the correct form using **-ing**.

a. sit – _____   c. cry – _____

b. write – _____   d. close – _____

2 Choose three verbs from activity 1. Then, in your notebook, write three sentences in the Present Continuous tense: one **affirmative**, one **negative** and one **interrogative**.

UNIT 2

Simple Present

O **Simple Present** é o tempo verbal usado para descrever fatos e ações habituais. Só há variação na 3ª pessoa do singular (**he, she, it**), quando é acrescentado o **s** ao verbo principal.

A forma afirmativa é composta de: sujeito + verbo + complemento (se houver).

Affirmative	I/You/We/You/They	sleep	early.
	He/She/It	sleeps	

A forma negativa é composta de: sujeito + do/does + not + verbo na forma básica + complemento (se houver).

Negative	I/You/We/You/They	do not (don't)	sleep early.
	He/She/It	does not (doesn't)	

A forma interrogativa é composta de: do/does + sujeito + verbo na forma básica + complemento (se houver).

Interrogative	Do	I/you/we/you/they	sleep early?
	Does	he/she/it	

1 Complete the sentences with the verbs in parentheses in the Simple Present.

a. James _____ to wear his blue sneakers. (like)

b. My friends _____ to wear a uniform at school. (not have)

c. Carol _____ to the movies on weekdays. (not go)

d. Mary _____ very well. (sing)

e. We _____ Science to Literature. (prefer)

2 In your notebook, write three sentences in the Simple Present: one **affirmative**, one **negative** and one **interrogative**.

UNIT 3

Simple Present (verb + to + verb)

Quando há dois verbos na mesma frase, eles se conectam pela partícula **to**. O primeiro verbo é o principal, e o segundo, com a partícula **to**, está no infinitivo, ou seja, em sua forma natural, sem conjugações.

Affirmative	I/You/We/You/They	want	to have	toast for breakfast.
	He/She/It	wants		

Na forma negativa, adicionamos o auxiliar *do* ou *does*, seguido de *not* (**don't** ou **doesn't**), apenas ao verbo principal, ou seja, ao primeiro verbo.

Negative	I **don't** want **to** cook tonight.
	She **doesn't** want **to** have soup for dinner.

Na forma interrogativa, adicionamos o auxiliar **do** ou **does** ao início da frase.

Interrogative	**Do** you prefer **to** have coffee or juice for breakfast? **Does** Kevin want **to** go to the supermarket?

1 Write sentences using the cues given.

a. for dinner/to/some red meat/buy/I/want

_____

b. cook/does/to/like/mother/your

_____

c. eat/prefer/a salad/to/I/lunch/for

_____

2 Answer the questions about yourself. Write full answers.

a. Do you prefer to have toast or eggs for breakfast?

_____

b. What kind of chocolate do you like to eat?

_____

c. What do you want to eat for dinner tonight?

_____

Object pronouns

Os **object pronouns** são pronomes oblíquos, normalmente usados após um verbo ou preposição. Veja o quadro a seguir, que apresenta a correspondência entre os *subject pronouns* e os *object pronouns*.

Subject pronouns	I	you	he	she	it	we	you	they
Object pronouns	me	you	him	her	it	us	you	them

> Suzy is going home with her friends. Suzy is going with **them**.
> Peter always gives **me** a book as a birthday present.

3 Complete the sentences with the correct object pronouns.

a. These are the new Geography teachers. I like _____.

b. That boy over there is my cousin. I live with _____.

c. My dog is intelligent. I love _____ very much.

Would + like

A combinação de would com o verbo **like** é usada para expressar com polidez preferências, fazer convites, pedidos e ofertas.

Interrogative	**Would** you **like** to order your meal?	What **would** you **like** to cook for dinner?
Affirmative	Yes, I **would**.	I **would like** to have a salad and a soup.
Negative	No, I **wouldn't**.	I **wouldn't like** to have dinner today.

4 Complete the sentences with **would like** or **wouldn't like**.

a. I _____ to have some orange juice, please.

b. Jim _____ to eat seafood because he is allergic to it.

c. My parents _____ to visit Kenya. They don't like hot weather.

d. I _____ to visit London one day. It is one of my dreams!

UNIT 4

Can/Could

O verbo modal *can* é usado em diversas situações, assim como seu passado, **could**. Para formular frases utilizando esses modais, seguimos as estruturas mostradas a seguir.

	Sujeito	Verbo modal	Verbo principal	Complemento (se houver)
Affirmative	I	can/could	run	fast.
Negative	He	cannot (can't)/ could not (couldn't)	run	fast.
Interrogative	Can/Could	you	run	fast?

1 Write sentences using the cues given.

a. you/ride/bike/not/can/your/now/.

_____

b. can/well/sing/dance/Mary/and/very/.

_____

c. line/could/wait/in/you/?

_____

d. if/we/watch/movie,/a/could/like/you/.

_____

Uses of can/could

Os verbos *can* e *could* são utilizados em diversas situações, como indica o quadro a seguir.

General ability	*Can* e *could* podem ser usados para **indicar habilidade**, sendo *can* usado para habilidades presentes e *could* para habilidades passadas.	I **can** drive well. I **could** drive well when I was younger.
Ask for permission	*Can* e *could* podem ser usados para **pedir permissão**, sendo *can* mais informal e *could* mais formal, educado.	**Can** I have your attention, please? **Could** I have your attention, please?
Make requests	*Can* e *could* podem ser usados para **fazer pedidos**, sendo *can* mais informal e *could* mais formal, educado.	**Can** you open the door, please? **Could** you close the window, please?
Express possibility	*Can* pode ser usado para **expressar possibilidade**.	It **can** rain any time today.
Offer help	*Can* pode ser usado para **oferecer ajuda**.	**Can** I help you with your bags?
Suggestion	*Could* pode ser usado para expressar uma **sugestão**.	We **could** go to the beach.

2 Complete the sentences with **can**, **can't**, **could** or **couldn't**.

a. I _____ swim when I was 5 years old, but now I _____.

b. _____ I help you? You look lost.

c. I think I'm sick. I _____ go to school today.

d. I know you don't like this restaurant. We _____ go to another one if you prefer.

e. Mom, _____ I eat a cookie, please?

Wh- questions – Question words

Para fazer perguntas específicas, cujas respostas vão além de *yes* ou *no*, usamos *question words*. Essas perguntas costumam ser chamadas de *Wh- questions*, pois as palavras que iniciam as perguntas geralmente começam com as letras *wh*.

Why can't she watch TV? Because she is studying.	**What** is her favorite school subject? Her favorite school subject is Art.	**Where** are the students? They are in the classroom.	**Who** is this woman? She is our new English teacher.

3 Complete the sentences below with the correct question word.

a. _____ is this artist's name? It's Pablo Picasso.

b. _____ is Pablo Picasso from? He's from Spain.

c. _____ is she? She's Frida Kahlo.

d. _____ can't we go to the movies? Because it's raining cats and dogs.

UNIT 5

Verb to be – Simple Past

	Sujeito	Verbo *to be*	Complemento
Affirmative	I/He/She/It	was	at home yesterday.
	You/We/You/They	were	
	Sujeito	Verbo *to be* + not	Complemento
Negative	I/He/She/It	was not (wasn't)	at home yesterday.
	You/We/You/They	were not (weren't)	
	Verbo *to be*	Sujeito	Complemento
Interrogative	Was	I/he/she/it	at home yesterday?
	Were	you/we/you/they	

Time expressions

Podem-se usar expressões de tempo para indicar que a frase está no passado. Veja o quadro a seguir.

last	last night, last Tuesday, last week, last month, last year
ago	ten minutes ago/two hours ago/five days ago
yesterday	yesterday morning/afternoon/evening

1 In your notebook, write three sentences: one **affirmative**, one **negative** and one **interrogative**. Use the verb to be in the Simple Past and time expressions.

2 Choose the correct option to complete the sentences below.

a. My grandfather _____ an engineer at an important company. (**was/were**)

b. _____ people happy with their new product? (**were/wasn't**)

c. Students _____ taking a test one hour ago. (**were/was**)

d. I _____ at home yesterday evening. (**weren't/wasn't**)

Prepositions of time

As preposições de tempo têm como objetivo indicar o tempo de uma ação: **in**, **on** e **at**.

In	Usada para indicar meses, anos, estações do ano e períodos do dia.	She was born **in April**. I went to the USA **in 2017**. He goes to Spain **in winter**. They go to school **in the morning**.
On	Usada para indicar dias da semana e dias específicos.	Roger plays tennis **on Wednesdays**. The wedding is **on Saturday morning**. My course started **on March 8th, 2019**. Mila studies a lot **on the weekend** (American English).
At	Usada para indicar horários, as expressões, **day**, **midday**, **night** e **midnight** e datas comemorativas.	Chris arrived at home **at 7:45 p.m**. The movie starts **at midnight**. I will go to a party **at Halloween**. Caio plays basketball **at the weekends** (British English).

3 Complete the following sentences with the correct prepositions of time.

a. Oh, no! I have a test _____ Monday morning and I forgot to study!

b. My birthday is _____ February. What about yours?

c. At what time does the rock concert start? It starts _____ 9 o'clock.

d. I can play videogames _____ night.

e. My mother was born _____ 1984.

UNIT 6

Simple Past – Regular Verbs

O *Simple Past* indica uma ação ou situação concluída no passado.

A forma afirmativa do Simple Past com verbos regulares é composta de: sujeito + verbo terminado em **-ed** + complemento (se houver).

Affirmative	I/You/He/She/It We/You/They	work**ed**	in the fields yesterday.

Nessa forma, o *Simple Past* com verbos regulares é composto de: sujeito + **did** + **not** + verbo na forma básica + complemento (se houver).

Negative	I/You/He/She/It We/You/They	did not/didn't	work	in the fields yesterday.

Na forma interrogativa o *Simple Past* com verbos regulares é composto de: **did** + sujeito + verbo na forma básica + complemento (se houver).

Interrogative	Did	I/you/he/she/it we/you/they	work	in the fields yesterday?

1. Para verbos terminados em **e**, adiciona-se apenas o **d**.
   escape – My dog escape**d** from the house yesterday.
2. Para verbos terminados em **y** e antecedidos por uma vogal, adiciona-se **ed**.
   enjoy – Peter and I enjoy**ed** the Avengers movie last Sunday.
3. Para verbos terminados em **y** e antecedidos por consoante, remove-se o **y** e adiciona-se **ied**.
   try – They tr**ied** to fly to London last night, but it was stormy.
4. Para verbos terminados em **consoante – vogal – consoante**, dobra-se a última consoante e adiciona-se **ed**.
   plan – I plan**ned** to cook for my friends last night.

1 Write the verbs below in the correct form using **-ed**.

a. terrify – _____   c. decide – _____

b. stop – _____   d. fry – _____

2 Complete the sentences below with the verbs in the parentheses. Use the Simple Past tense.

a. I _____ soccer with my friends last week. (play)

b. Mary, _____ in the party? The music selection was nice. (dance)

c. I _____ the game last night. It was really boring! (not like)

d. My father _____ yesterday. We ordered pizza for dinner. (not cook)

Simple Past – Short answers

Para responder de forma curta, usa-se apenas o sujeito seguido de **did** ou **didn't**.

Did you go to the mall last night?	
Affirmative	Yes, I **did**.
Negative	No, I **didn't**.

3 In pairs, ask the following questions. Then report his/her answers to your classmates.

a. Did your family have a special dinner last weekend?
_____

b. Did you practice any sports last month?
_____

c. Did you listen to any music this morning?
_____

Quantifiers – Some and any

Para expressar uma quantidade indefinida de algo, usam-se as palavras **some** e **any**.

Em frases afirmativas usa-se o **some**, que é também utilizado em frases interrogativas quando algo é oferecido ou solicitado.

Affirmative	Interrogative (offer or request)
There are **some** cars parked there.	Would you like **some** water?

Em frases negativas e interrogativas, em geral, usa-se a palavra **any**.

Negative	Interrogative
There aren't **any** cars parked there.	Are there **any** cars parked there?

4 Complete the text with **some** or **any**.

Yesterday there was a party at Phill´s house. There were lots of people, and _____ of them were his friends from school. There was music and _____ people danced all night long. After singing happy birthday, there was _____ cake and sweets for us to eat, but there wasn't _____ soda, only juice to drink. It was really fun!

Countable and uncountable nouns – Many/Much/A lot of

Para perguntar a quantidade de algo, usamos **how much** e **how many**. Com substantivos contáveis (*countables*), usamos *how many*, ao passo que, com substantivos incontáveis (*uncountables*), usamos *how much*. Para responder a essas perguntas, usamos *many*, *much* ou a *lot of*.

Uncountable	Countable
How much flour do we need to bake the cake? Not **much**. We have a **lot of** flour in the pantry.	**How many** apples do we have in the fridge? I have **many** apples in the fridge. I have **a lot of** apples in the fridge.

5 Complete the sentences with **much** or **many**.

a. My mother doesn't drink _____ coffee in the morning.

b. Lucas has _____ pairs of shoes. He has about 100 pairs!

c. I try not to eat _____ chocolate on weekdays.

UNIT 7

Simple Past – Irregular verbs

Os verbos irregulares no passado não possuem um padrão de conjugação, como mostra o quadro de verbos da página 150.

Na forma afirmativa, é importante estar atento à forma irregular de cada verbo.

Affirmative	I/You/He/She/It	**went** to bed late yesterday.
	We/You/They	

Na negativa, adiciona-se **didn't** após o sujeito e o verbo volta à forma básica.

Negative	I/You/He/She/It	**didn't go** to bed late yesterday.
	We/You/They	

Na interrogativa, o **did** vem no início da frase após o sujeito e o verbo na forma básica.

Interrogative	Did	I/you/he/she/it	**go** to bed late yesterday?
		we/you/they	

UNIT 8
Past Continuous

O *Past Continuous* expressa ações em andamento em determinado período no passado. Sua estrutura é composta de: verbo **to be** no passado + verbo principal terminado em **-ing**. Veja os exemplos a seguir.

> I **was sleeping** at 9 o'clock last night.
> The kids **were listening** to music yesterday.

1 Complete the sentences using the Past Continuous form of the given verbs.

a. I _____ at Susan's party last month. (dance)

b. _____ for your friends at the concert hall? (wait)

c. I _____ TV last night. (not watch)

Para indicar que uma ação estava em andamento (*Past Continuous*) quando outra ocorreu (*Simple Past*), usamos *when* ou *while*. Já para sinalizar que duas ações estavam acontecendo ao mesmo tempo, usamos apenas *while*. Veja o quadro a seguir.

Affirmative	Karen **was watching** TV when she **texted** me.
Negative	When Mark **called**, we **weren't** having dinner.
Interrogative	**Was** Lilly **working** while Louis called her?

2 Complete the sentences with **when** or **while**.

a. _____ I was watching TV, my dad was making a sandwich.

b. I was sitting in the bus _____ the accident happened.

c. My dog ran away _____ I was walking him.

d. I was opening my umbrella _____ it started to rain.

WORKBOOK

NAME: _____

CLASS: _____ DATE: _____

UNIT 1 – STUDYING ABROAD

1 Read the dialog and complete the gaps using the words and expressions from the box.

> abroad   benefits   Cartagena   culture
> exchange   hamburger   my friend   new language   nice

Matt: Hi, Janet! Long time no see!

Janet: Hi, Matt. This is _____ Paola Ruiz. She is from _____, in Colombia.

Matt: _____ to meet you, Paola! Do you go to school here, too?

Paola: Just for one semester. I am an _____ student.

Matt: Awesome! Tell me, Paola, what are the benefits of studying _____?

Paola: Well, there are many _____. But the most important, in my opinion, is that we can make lifelong friends, learn a _____ and develop a new perspective of our own _____.

Janet: Paola, you forgot something! What about the food? I know you love our eating habits!

Paola: You are right! I love pumpkin pie, Texas barbecue, green bean casserole, roast turkey, and the most delicious food in the world, _____!

Matt: So, what about a hamburger tonight at Spark's?

Janet and Paola: We are in!

2 Besides the benefits of studying abroad mentioned by Paola, what else can you add? Read the options below and check the ones you consider a benefit that this experience could bring into your life.

○ Watch interesting celebrations.   ○ Visit tourist attractions.

○ Personal growth.   ○ Others: _____

ONE HUNDRED AND SIXTY-ONE 161

3 Think of the school subjects you are studying and complete with information about yourself.

I'm great at: _____

I do OK at: _____

I'm not so good at: _____

4 Write full sentences using the Present Continuous. Then match them to the corresponding pictures. There is one extra picture.

a. The athlete from Jamaica/win/the race. (affirmative)
_____

b. Chef Karmal/have a barbecue./He/bake/bread. (negative – affirmative)
_____

c. The Smiths/swim./They/watch/a movie at home. (negative – affirmative)
_____

d. Kids/ride their bicycles. (interrogative – affirmative)
_____

WORKBOOK

NAME: _____

CLASS: _____ DATE: _____

UNIT 2 – THE SUSTAINABLE GENERATION

1 Look at the pictures and match them to the corresponding words.

a. [shirt image]   b. [t-shirt image]   c. [skirt image]

○ skirt
○ dress shirt
○ T-shirt

2 Check the correct alternatives to complete the dialog below.

Morgana, Jack and Pilar are friends. They were at the mall when suddenly...

Morgana: Look! Isn't that girl Amelia Fox?

Pilar: Where? What is she (a) _____?

Morgana: She is in that clothing store over there. She is wearing a short (b) _____ and a white T-shirt.

Jack: Who is Amelia Fox?

Pilar: That famous girl who (c) _____ "Dancing in the Sky".

Jack: That girl doesn't sing, she (d) _____!

Morgana: Come on, Jack! Amelia Fox sings very well!

Jack: You wish! By the way, Amelia Fox (e) _____ skirts. She only wears (f) _____ and T-shirts all the time.

Pilar: Look at the cover of this magazine, Jack! I'm sorry, but you are wrong! She (g) _____ skirts!

Morgana: Look, guys... that girl (h) _____ Amelia Fox.

a. ○ wears   ○ wearing   e. ○ don't wear   ○ doesn't wear
b. ○ skirt   ○ jeans   f. ○ jeans   ○ skirt
c. ○ sings   ○ sing   g. ○ wear   ○ wears
d. ○ shouting   ○ shouts   h. ○ isn't   ○ aren't

ONE HUNDRED AND SIXTY-THREE

3 Read the dialog in activity 2 again and check the correct Amelia Fox's magazine cover.

a.

b.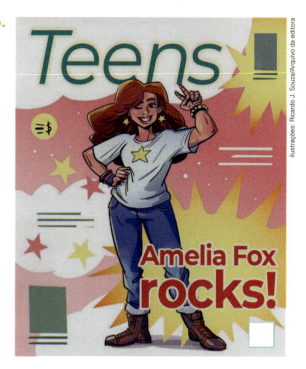

4 Imagine that you are in a clothing store and want to try on some clothes. Write a dialog between you and the salesperson. After that, glue or draw your outfit.

WORKBOOK

NAME: _____

CLASS: _____ DATE: _____

UNIT 3 – CAN I HAVE THE MENU, PLEASE?

1 Match the people to their orders. Consider **M** for Mayara and **D** for David. There are some extra pictures.

At the restaurant…

Mayara: I would like to eat some spaghetti and meatballs. What about you, David?

David: Well, I'm on a diet, so I will order just a small bowl of tomato soup and a glass of water.

Mayara: You are kidding! No dessert?

David: I could eat a slice of brownie, but my answer is no!

Mayara: I hope you don't mind, but that is exactly what I'm going to order for dessert with a scoop of vanilla ice cream!

David: Oh, please! That's so mean, Mayara!

a. 　b. 　c.

d. 　e. 　f.

ONE HUNDRED AND SIXTY-FIVE　**165**

2 Answer the following question using the structure **verb + to + verb**.

a. What do you prefer to eat for lunch?

_____

_____

_____

3 Complete the following dialogs with **me**, **him**, **her**, **it**, **us** or **them**.

a. **A:** Do you like Lady Gaga?

B: I do like _____, but I prefer Shakira.

b. **A:** Who is that man over there?

B: I don't know _____.

c. **A:** Tell _____, Marie, when do you do your homework?

B: I usually do _____ in the afternoon.

d. **A:** Chris, did you buy the vegetables that I need?

B: Yes, I bought _____ all. What are you going to cook?

A: Spanish vegetable soup. I know you love it!

e. **A:** Is that girl Dan's sister?

B: Yes. I don't like _____. She is so bossy.

A: Dan is very bossy, too!

B: You are right. I don't like _____ at all.

A: Well, I think they don't like _____ either.

4 Write questions to the answers below.

a. _____

I would like to travel to Hawaii.

b. _____

I would like to surf and practice Hula dance there.

c. _____

I would like to eat poke, a traditional Hawaiian dish.

WORKBOOK

NAME: _____

CLASS: _____ DATE: _____

UNIT 4 – ENJOYING ART

1 Look at the pictures below and label them according to the artistic expression they represent.

a.

b.

_____

c.

d.

_____

e.

f.

_____

g.

h.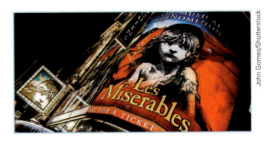

_____

2 Which forms of artistic expression mentioned in activity 1 do you prefer? Why?

_____
_____

3 Read Sandy's e-mail and complete the gaps with **can**, **can't**, **could** or **couldn't**.

> From: Sandy
> To: Matt
> Subject: Good news!
>
> Hi, Matt. How's it going?
>
> Here is the news. I love my current job as an English teacher at St. Peter's School.
>
> I _____ go to the language lab with my students anytime I want. I _____ do that when I was a teacher at Long Island's School.
>
> To be honest, I miss Long Island's School a little bit. There I _____ take my students to the public park nearby, but at St. Peter's I _____ go outside with them because of the distance between the school and the park. On the other hand, the salary range here is higher!
>
> Guess what? I'm attending a painting course, so I _____ improve my techniques!
>
> 😜 You know that when I was a teenager I _____ paint very well, right? LoL
>
> Well, tell mom I'll call her later.
>
> XOXO
>
> Sandy

4 Now write sentences about things that you **can** and **can't** do. Also write about things that you **could** and **couldn't** do when you were younger. Use the clues below to guide you.

At school.

_____
_____

At home.

_____
_____

In your free time.

_____
_____

WORKBOOK

NAME: _____

CLASS: _____ DATE: _____

UNIT 5 – WEATHER CONDITIONS

1 Read João Pedro's e-mail and check the correct words to complete it.

From: João Pedro
To: Carlo
Subject: Lisbon, I love it!

Hi, Carlo. How are you?

I have some pretty good news! I'm living in Lisbon now. Can you believe it?

Julia and I are in love with the city and the food. Now it's winter here and the temperature is really (1) _____, but people say that (2) _____ in Lisbon is very hot. We are lucky because it's (3) _____ today, so we are going to visit Mosteiro dos Jerônimos (Jeronimos Monastery) and then have a picnic in a park near here. I am sending you a picture of it.

Winter in Lisbon is in (4) _____, January and (5) _____. So different from Brazil! By the way, your sister told me that you (6) _____ in Pernambuco last month. I (7) _____ there, too!

What about visiting me in Lisbon?

Send hugs to everyone! Talk to you later!
João Pedro

	February	was	were	summer	cold	sunny	December
1							
2							
3							
4							
5							
6							
7							

2 Fill in the gaps using the verb **to be** in the past form.

a. **A:** Hey, Tom. Where is Mandy?

B: I don't know where she is now, but she _____ in the library 20 minutes ago.

A: _____ she alone?

B: No, she _____. She _____ with Pamela.

b. **A:** Jack, where _____ you and your brother last night? I _____ so worried, guys.

B: We _____ at the sports club, mom.

A: I forgot that! Sorry! _____ your sister with you?

B: No, mom, she _____. She is at Christina's. You forgot that, too!

A: Oh, my God! I'm sorry again!

3 Imagine that you are living abroad. Write an e-mail to a friend and tell him/her about the country you are living in. What is the weather like there? How is the temperature? What are the months of the seasons? What are the things that you enjoy doing?

From:
To:
Subject:

WORKBOOK

NAME: _____

CLASS: _____ DATE: _____

UNIT 6 – IT WAS AN AMAZING PARTY!

1 Read the dialog and check the party supplies that were mentioned.

Anna: Hello!

Josh: Hi, Anna! This is Josh. Is everything alright about the surprise party to teacher Vera?

Anna: Well, I think so. I ordered the cake and the cupcakes.

Josh: Do we have any juice?

Anna: Jack will buy the juice and the plastic plates.

Josh: Is he in charge of the plastic forks, too?

Anna: No, Carla is. Her sister, Bia, is going to bring the sandwiches.

Josh: Great! How much money do we still have left?

Anna: Only 22 dollars.

Josh: Don't we have any extra money?

Anna: Yes, we have some extra money to buy the present. Why?

Josh: Yesterday, Andrew and I planned to buy some balloons and some candles.

Anna: Great idea! You can take the 22 dollars!

a.

b.

c.

d.

2 Now, answer the questions. Write full answers.

a. Did Josh order the cake?

_____

b. Do they have any extra money left? What is the extra money for?

_____

c. What did Josh and Andrew plan?

_____

d. How much money do they still have to buy the party supplies?

_____

3. Write the verbs in the past form in the correct column.

	-ed	-ied	Double the last letter + ed
watch			
plan			
marry			
play			
stop			

4. Now use some of the verbs from the previous activity to complete the following dialogs.

a. **A:** Last night, David and I _____ a romantic movie.

   B: Which movie _____ you _____?

   A: We _____ A Star Is Born.

b. **A:** Tell me, Sarah, when _____ you _____ eating red meat?

   B: I _____ last year, after my birthday. When _____ you _____ eating red meat?

   A: I _____ eating red meat. I _____ eating gluten.

c. **A:** What sports _____ you _____ at your old school?

   B: I _____ volleyball and soccer.

   A: _____ you _____ any other sports?

   B: No, I _____ any other sports.

5. Now write one more dialog using the verbs left.

_____
_____
_____
_____
_____

WORKBOOK

NAME: _____

CLASS: _____ DATE: _____

UNIT 7 – DID YOU KNOW…?

1 Read the definitions below. Find the names of the inventions in the wordsearch and write them in the correct place.

a. _____ : A piece of equipment that is used to talk to someone who is in another place.

b. _____ : A vehicle designed for air travel that has wings and engines.

c. _____ : A device with a viewing screen on the front, used for watching programmes, cartoons, soap operas etc.

d. _____ : A piece of electronic equipment for playing games on.

e. _____ : A device with parts that cover each ear through which you can listen to something, such as music, without other people hearing.

f. _____ : An electronic machine that calculates data very quickly, used for storing, writing, organizing, and sharing information electronically or for controlling other machines.

g. _____ : A device for taking photographs, making films, or recording images on videotape.

C	A	M	E	R	A	T	L	A	F	I	O	V	Y	T
O	L	G	B	A	S	E	O	R	R	G	N	U	M	A
M	E	T	U	T	E	L	V	I	S	I	O	N	N	I
P	H	N	I	D	G	E	T	S	A	V	O	S	C	R
U	H	H	E	A	D	P	H	O	N	E	S	G	C	P
T	T	S	A	V	Q	H	E	I	H	E	V	Z	U	L
E	Q	F	Z	W	Q	O	I	N	E	D	S	W	U	A
R	P	D	K	Ç	M	N	H	D	P	Q	T	K	D	N
Y	U	P	G	A	M	E	•	C	O	N	S	O	L	E

2. Read about two important inventions. Then complete the gaps with the past tense of the verbs from the box. There is one extra verb.

find   make   take

a.

Phonograph – 1877

Thomas Edison _____ that sound could be captured and replayed using a rotating cylinder covered with paraffin paper and a stylus. In December 1888, Edison applied for a patent and over the next few years helped to develop the modern gramophone based on the wax-cylinder model.

b.

Box Camera – 1888

George Eastman developed the first small Kodak box camera which _____ photography much more accessible to the public.

Available at: <www.biographyonline.net/scientists/modern-inventions.html>. Accessed on: Mar. 6, 2019.

3. Look at the cartoon attentively and check the text that best suits the blank space.

Available at: <www.glasbergen.com>. Accessed on: Mar. 6, 2019.

a. ◯ Your grandmother sent you $5 for your birthday.

b. ◯ Your grandmother didn't send you $5 for your birthday.

4. Complete the sentences below using the verbs given in the correct tense. Use affirmative, negative or interrogative forms according to the context of each situation.

a. I _____ pizza last night. Tom did! (buy)

b. Mom _____ all night just to arrive to the party on time. (drive)

c. I _____ a strange noise last night. _____ you _____ that too? (hear)

d. Daniel _____ asleep 10 minutes ago. He _____ extremely tired. (fall/be)

e. **A:** Sandy, help me! I _____ my keys! (lose – go)

   B: Where _____ you _____ them?

   A: One hour ago, I _____ to the bakery. Maybe the keys are there!

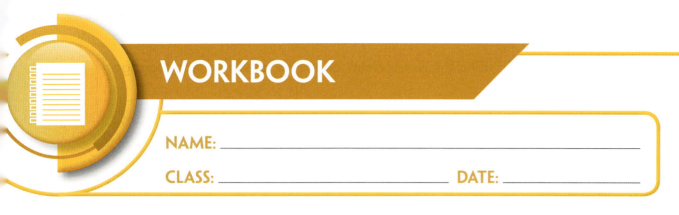

UNIT 8 – WHAT TIME WAS SAYURI'S FLIGHT?

1 Read some instructions about checking in at an airport. Then fill in the gaps with the words from the box.

> airline   boarding pass   check-in   departure   flight   gate

What to look out for

_____ times vary from _____ to airline, so it is advisable to check in well in advance of your _____ date. Once you know about how much time to leave before checking in, you will need to factor in how much time you need to get through security and reach the departure _____ with plenty of time to board your _____. [...]

Check-in online

Many airlines offer the option of being able to check in online (and some only allow online check-in). If you check in online, you will either have to print out your _____ or, in some cases, you will have it on your mobile phone. [...]

Available at: <www.caa.co.uk/Passengers/At-the-airport/Checking-in-and-security/>. Accessed on: Mar. 6, 2019.

2 Use some words from activity 1 to complete the dialogs below.

a. **A:** Can you confirm the time of my _____, please?
   B: Sure, sir. You are scheduled to depart at 5:00 p.m.

b. **A:** Can I check your _____, please?
   B: Sure. Here it is.

c. **A:** Can you tell me the _____ number to Rome by Italian Airlines?
   B: It is 11-B, sir.

d. **A:** How can I do the online _____ using my cell phone?
   B: You can find instructions at the counter on your left, sir.

ONE HUNDRED AND SEVENTY-FIVE 175

3 Create a short dialog using the words **claim**, **conveyor**, **passport**, and **luggage**.

___

4 Write sentences using the cues given.

a. Craig/fall asleep/watch TV last night (while)

___

b. My sister/go to the beach every day/be in Cancun (when)

___

c. The rock concert/begin/it start to rain (when)

___

d. I/cook a surprise dinner/dad/walk into the kitchen (while)

___

5 Write one meaningful sentence for each of the linking words below to exemplify their use.

Linking words	Idea indicated	Sentences
Then	Sequence	
But	Contrast	
Because	Cause	
When	Time	

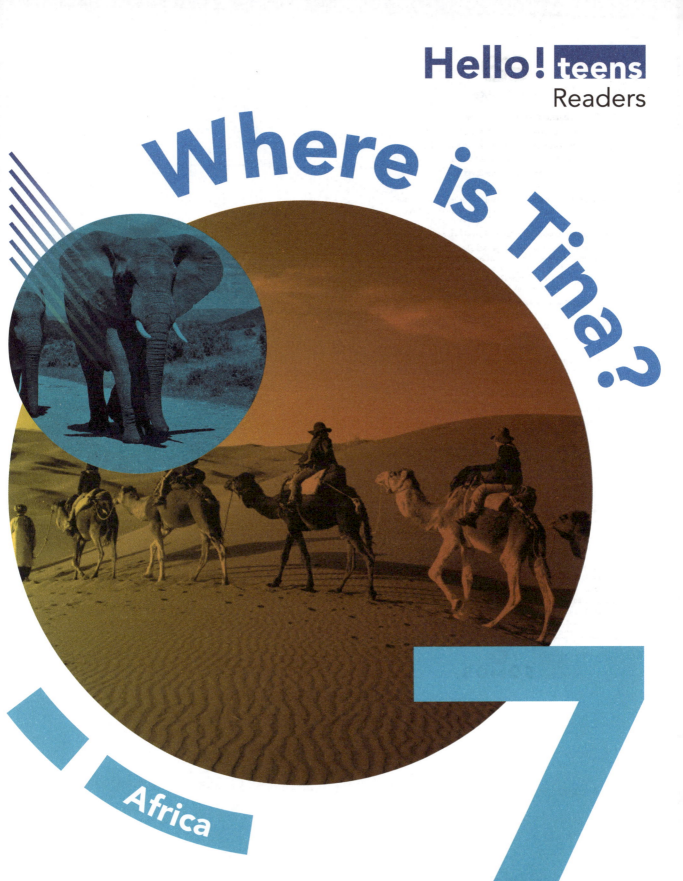

Direção Presidência: Mario Ghio Júnior
Direção de Conteúdo e Operações: Wilson Troque
Direção editorial: Luiz Tonolli e Lidiane Vivaldini Olo
Gestão de projeto editorial: Mirian Senra
Gestão de área: Alice Silvestre
Coordenação: Renato Malkov
Edição: Ana Lucia Militello, Carla Fernanda Nascimento (assist.), Caroline Santos, Danuza Dias Gonçalves, Maiza Prande Bernardello, Milena Rocha (assist.), Sabrina Cairo Bileski
Planejamento e controle de produção: Patrícia Eiras e Adjane Queiroz
Revisão: Hélia de Jesus Gonsaga (ger.), Kátia Scaff Marques (coord.), Rosângela Muricy (coord.), Ana Curci, Ana Paula C. Malfa, Arali Gomes, Brenda T. M. Morais, Diego Carbone, Gabriela M. Andrade, Luís M. Boa Nova, Patricia Cordeiro; Amanda T. Silva e Bárbara de M. Genereze (estagiárias)
Arte: Daniela Amaral (ger.), Catherine Saori Ishihara (coord.) e Letícia Lavôr (edit. arte)
Iconografia e tratamento de imagem: Sílvio Kligin (ger.), Claudia Bertolazzi (coord.), Evelyn Torrecilla (pesquisa iconográfica), Cesar Wolf e Fernanda Crevin (tratamento)
Licenciamento de conteúdos de terceiros: Thiago Fontana (coord.), Flavia Zambon e Angra Marques (licenciamento de textos), Erika Ramires, Luciana Pedrosa Bierbauer, Luciana Cardoso Sousa e Claudia Rodrigues (analistas adm.)
Ilustrações: Igor RAS
Cartografia: Eric Fuzii (coord.), Robson Rosendo da Rocha (edit. arte)
Design: Gláucia Koller (ger.), Talita Guedes (proj. gráfico e capa), Luis Vassallo (capa) e Gustavo Vanini (assist. arte)
Foto de capa: Yongyut Kumsri/Shutterstock e Michael Potter11/Shutterstock

Todos os direitos reservados por Editora Ática S.A.
Avenida das Nações Unidas, 7221, 3º andar, Setor A
Pinheiros – São Paulo – SP – CEP 05425-902
Tel.: 4003-3061
www.atica.com.br / editora@atica.com.br

2020
Código da obra CL 742203
CAE 648311 (AL) / 648310 (PR)
8ª edição
3ª impressão
De acordo com a BNCC.

Impressão e acabamento EGB Editora Gráfica Bernardi Ltda

Uma publicação

#DAY1
CAPE TOWN, SOUTH AFRICA

Asking for Directions

Tina: Excuse me. How can I get to the Castle of Good Hope, please?

Taxi driver: Walk four blocks and turn right. Then walk one block and turn left. The Castle is on your right.

Tina: Are you free now, sir?

Taxi driver: Yes, I am.

Tina: Can you drive me there now?

Taxi driver: Of course.

Tina: Great! Let's go. But not too fast, I'm not in a hurry. I'm just on vacation!

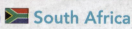 **South Africa**
Capital: Cape Town (legislative)/ Bloemfontein (judicial)/ Pretoria (administrative)
Location: South Africa
Area: 1,219,089 sq. km
Population: 57,975,670
Currency: Rand
Languages: Afrikaans, English, Ndebele, Sotho etc.
Nationality: South African

Cape Town

 **CROSS CULTURAL**

Nelson Mandela (1918-2013) helped to end apartheid (it means "apartness" in Afrikaans), a racist system, in 1994. Afrikaans is one of the eleven official languages spoken in South Africa.

CAPE OF GOOD HOPE, SOUTH AFRICA.

1 Read and answer the questions.

   a. What is the meaning of the word "apartheid" in Afrikaans?

   b. How many official languages are there in South Africa?

2 Underline the correct alternative to complete the sentences.

   a. Cape Town is in **Europe/Africa**.

   b. The **taxi driver/travel agent** is giving Tina some information.

   c. Tina is asking for directions to go to **the Castle of Good Hope/the hotel**.

   d. Tina is **in a hurry/on vacation**.

3 Read Tina's e-mail about South Africa's safari.

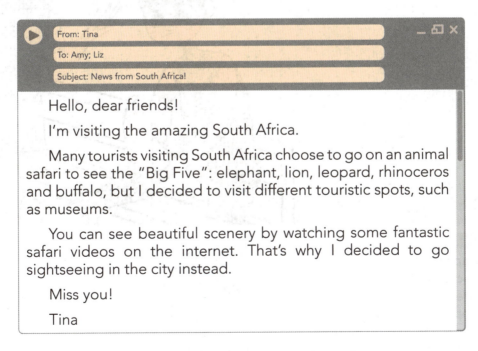

4 Now, write the name of the animals you can find on a safari.

#DAY29

PORT LOUIS, MAURITIUS

Tina Goes Snorkeling

Tina: So, here I am.

Instructor: Is this your first time snorkeling?

Tina: Yes. I'm very excited.

Instructor: Good! You are going to see many beautiful things.

Tina: I can't wait!

Instructor: But you have to follow my instructions to be safe and have a good time.

Tina: OK. Are we going to see the reefs?

Instructor: Sure. The coral reefs are covering all the ocean floor in this area.

Tina: Wow!

Instructor: And you'll see lots of different fish as well. Let's go!

 **Mauritius**
Capital: Port Louis
Location: East Africa
Area: 2,040 sq. km
Population: 1,270,984
Currency: Mauritian rupee
Languages: English, French and Creole
Nationality: Mauritian

The Republic of Mauritius is a group of islands and archipelagos in the Indian Ocean comprising Mauritius, Rodrigues, Agalega, Tromelin, Cargados Carajos (Saint Brandon) and the Chagos Archipelago, including Diego Garcia. Mauritius is the main island, and the most known for tourism.

MAURITIUS

1 Write **T** (True) or **F** (False).

a. ◯ Tina is going to see the coral reef.

b. ◯ She is going to go snorkeling for the first time.

c. ◯ The instructor is not going to help Tina.

d. ◯ Tina is going to see a lot of different fish.

2 Find words in the text on page 6 that mean the following.

a. very enthusiastic: _____

b. swim using a snorkel: _____

c. a very large expanse of sea: _____

3 Answer the questions.

a. Are there coral reefs in your country?
_____

b. Do you like going to the beach?
_____
_____

c. Would you like to go snorkeling? Why?
_____
_____
_____

#DAY42
ABUJA, NIGERIA

Feeling Sick

Doctor: Good morning, Ms. Traveler. How do you feel?

Tina: I'm feeling sick, doctor. *Cough, cough!*

Doctor: OK. Open your mouth. Let me see your throat.

Tina: *Aaaah.*

Doctor: You have a cold and a sore throat.

Tina: What can I do?

Doctor: Drink lots of liquids, go to bed and rest.

Tina: Can I go on a tour tomorrow?

Doctor: I suggest you get some rest, but if you feel better tomorrow, go for it.

Tina: OK, thank you, doctor.

 **Nigeria**
Capital: Abuja
Location: West Africa
Area: 923,763 sq. km
Population: 200,292,529
Currency: Naira
Languages: English and 520 other languages as Hausa, Yoruba, Igbo etc.
Nationality: Nigerian

 **CROSS CULTURAL**

The name "Nigeria" comes from the Niger River – that runs through the country. Nigeria is the most populous country in Africa and the eighth most populous country in the world. In some areas of Nigeria, ethnic groups speak more than one language. Nigeria's official language is English.

KANO CITY WALLS, NIGERIA.

1 Answer the following questions about Nigeria.

a. Where does the name "Nigeria" come from?
_____

b. Is English spoken in Nigeria?
_____

c. What is Brazil's official language?
_____

d. Which is the most populous city in Brazil?
_____

2 Match each word to its correct meaning.

a. rest   ◯ a drink

b. throat   ◯ period of sleep or not being active

c. tea   ◯ part of the body inside the neck

3 Complete the paragraph below with the words from the box.

| gold | sport | football | Championship | 3 times |

Football is Nigeria's national _____ and the country has its own Football Premier League. Nigeria's national _____ team, known as the Super Eagles, participated in the World Cup in 1994, 1998, 2002, 2010, 2014 and 2018, and won the African Cup of Nations _____.

Nigeria won the _____ medal for football in the 1996 Summer Olympics and reached the finals of the U-20 World _____ in 2005.

#DAY58

MARRAKESH, MOROCCO

Going Shopping

Salesperson: Good morning, ma'am. Can I help you?

Tina: Oh, yes, please. How much are the slippers?

Salesperson: They are six dirhams.

Tina: I like the blue ones.

Salesperson: Do you want to try them on?

Tina: Yes, please.

Salesperson: Here you are.

Tina: They're really comfortable.

Salesperson: They are, for sure.

Tina: I think I'll take the red ones, too.

Salesperson: Right. Do you need a bag?

Tina: No, thanks.

Salesperson: That's twelve dirhams.

Tina: Here you are. Thank you.

Salesperson: Have a great day!

Morocco
Capital: Rabat
Location: Northwest Africa
Area: 446,550 sq. km
Population: 36,575,733
Currency: Moroccan dirham
Languages: Arabic and Berber
Nationality: Moroccan

Mint tea is Morocco's national drink. This dates back to the 19th century when British merchants became stranded off the coast and had to offload their cargos. The Moroccan people have an authentic recipe for mint tea.

MOROCCAN MINT TEA.

1 Put the dialog in order.

a. ◯ I'll take the blue ones.

b. ◯ How much are the slippers?

c. ◯ No, thank you.

d. ◯ They're six dirhams.

e. ◯ Do you need a bag?

2 Underline the correct word to complete the sentences.

a. Do you **want/wanted** to try on the slippers?

b. They are **sure/really** comfortable.

c. How **many/much** are the slippers?

3 Complete the sentences with words from the text.

a. I'll _____ the blue ones.

b. Can I _____ you?

c. Have a _____ day!

#DAY73

CAIRO, EGYPT

A Camel Ride

Tour guide: May I help you, Miss?

Tina: Does this tour include a camel ride to the Pyramids of Giza?

Tour guide: Yes, and the other ancient Egyptian pyramids located nearby as well.

Tina: How much does it cost?

Tour guide: 70 Egyptian pounds.

Tina: How long does it take?

Tour guide: It takes about 4 hours. And we are leaving now.

Tina: Great! I am ready for this exciting adventure in the desert!

Tour guide: OK, this is your camel, get on it, please!

Tour guide: Now we are approaching the Great Pyramid of Giza, one of the most famous pyramids in the world and… Miss Traveler, are you OK?

Tina: Yes, sir! Sure!

 **Egypt**
Capital: Cairo
Location: North Africa
Area: 1,001,449 sq. km
Population: 100,927,887
Currency: Egyptian pound
Language: Arabic
Nationality: Egyptian

The Great Pyramid of Giza is the tallest one of the three pyramids of the Giza Necropolis complex and they are located 18 km away from the city of Cairo. It was built around 2560 BC as a tomb for the Pharaoh Khufu and it is the last remaining construction of the Seven Wonders of the Ancient World.

THE GIZA NECROPOLIS

1 Write **T** (True) or **F** (False).

a. ◯ The Pyramids of Giza is in the city of Cairo.

b. ◯ All the Seven Wonders of the Ancient World still exist.

c. ◯ The pyramid is a tomb for a pharaoh.

2 Correct the sentences according to the dialog on page 12.

a. Tina wants to visit the Great Sphinx of Giza.
_____

b. The tour costs 45 dollars.
_____

c. Tina is ready for a boring adventure in the desert.
_____

3 Fill in the blanks with the words from the box.

| wrapped | organs | Monastery | corpse | treasures |

A mummy is a _____ that was specially prepared to be buried. In the mummification process, the internal _____ were removed and the body was embalmed and _____ with strips of white linen. One of the most famous mummies is the Pharaoh Tutankhamun. His tomb was found in the beginning of the 20th century full of precious _____ that are now in the Egyptian Museum in Cairo. In 2008, two 200-year-old mummies were found in São Paulo, inside the walls of the Luz _____.

#DAY91

MAASAI MARA, KENYA

On a Safari

Guide: Good morning, everyone. Welcome to Maasai Mara National Reserve. In this tour, we're planning to see lions, leopards, cheetahs, buffalos and elephants.

Tina: Wow.

Guide: And if we're lucky, we can see the black rhino, too.

Tina: A black rhino?

Guide: Yes, it's an endangered species, and it's very rare. I think there are only 25 to 30 rhinos nowadays.

Tina: Oh, that's so sad.

Guide: I know. They are poached for their horns.

Tina: Really?

Guide: Yes, but our rangers are here to protect them.

Tina: That's good to know.

Guide: So now, let's start moving. Please keep your hands and legs always inside the vehicle and remain seated. And let me know if you have any questions about our fabulous animals.

 Kenya
Capital: Nairobi
Location: East Africa
Area: 580,370 sq. km
Population: 52,048,663
Currency: Kenyan shilling
Language: English, Swahili
Nationality: Kenyan

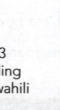

Maasai Mara National Reserve

CROSS CULTURAL

Most marathon runners from Kenya are from the same tribe, known as Kalenjin. Scientists and sports gurus tried to explain why people from Kalenjin are the best runners. They claim it can be their high-starch diet or the altitude, but in fact, none of them could explain why this particular tribe is so dominant.

KALENJIN ATHLETE.

1 Match the words to their correct meaning.

a. poached   ◯ a person whose job is to protect a forest

b. endangered   ◯ having good things happen by chance

c. lucky   ◯ to catch and kill animals without permission

d. rangers   ◯ animals or plants that may soon not exist

2 Answer the questions according to the dialog on page 14.

a. What is the name of the place where Tina is?
_____

b. Which animals can Tina see on the safari?
_____
_____

c. Why are the black rhinos poached?
_____
_____

d. What is the instruction the guide gives people in the vehicle?
_____
_____

3 Read the sentences below and check. What is true about your country?

a. ◯ There are endangered species.

b. ◯ The rangers protect the forests.

c. ◯ You can see black rhinos in their natural habitat.

#DAY145

KILIMANJARO, TANZANIA

Mountain Climbing

Tina: Wow, what a view!

Emma: Yes, Kilimanjaro is definitely a great mountain.

Tina: Is this your first time here?

Emma: No, it's my third time actually.

Tina: Really? So you're an expert.

Emma: No, no… I could never get to the summit.

Tina: Why not?

Emma: Well, the climbing is easy, because you don't need special equipment. You just need special and warm clothing. But as you go up, you have to deal with the altitude sickness. I tried to climb Kilimanjaro twice and I got sick because of the altitude.

Tina: Oh, really?

Emma: Yeah, let's see today. I hope I can make it to the summit.

Tina: Good luck!

Tanzania
Capital: Dodoma
Location: East Africa
Area: 947,300 sq. km
Population: 60,674,421
Currency: Tanzanian shilling
Language: Swahili, English
Nationality: Tanzanian

Mount Kilimanjaro

CROSS CULTURAL

Ngorongoro Crater, located in northern Tanzania, is thought to be the result of a volcanic explosion and is considered one of the best places to see the Big Five (African elephant, African lion, African leopard, Cape buffalo and black rhinoceros) if you go on a safari.

NGORONGORO CRATER, TANZANIA.

1 Read and answer the questions.

a. How do you call the top of a mountain?
_____

b. What do you usually need to climb a high mountain?
_____

c. What can stop you from reaching the top?
_____

2 Match the two parts of the sentences.

a. It's Emma's   ◯ she can reach the summit.

b. Kilimanjaro is   ◯ third time in Kilimanjaro.

c. Emma hopes   ◯ good luck.

d. Tina wishes Emma   ◯ a great mountain.

3 Underline the correct word to complete each sentence.

a. Kilimanjaro is in **Kenya/Tanzania**.

b. Tina likes the **view/climbing** of Kilimanjaro.

c. Tina thinks Emma is **a great person/an expert**.

PRASLIN, SEYCHELLES

Is it a Parrot?

Tina: Excuse me, sir. Is Seychelles an island or an archipelago?

Tour guide: Seychelles is an archipelago with 115 islands. The largest ones are Mahe and this one here, Praslin.

Tina: And what's that? Is it a parrot?

Tour guide: Oh, no. That's the *kato nwar*, or the black parrot as people call it.

Tina: It's very beautiful.

Tour guide: Yes, it is! It exists only on this island and it's protected by law.

Tina: That's very interesting.

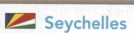 **Seychelles**
Capital: Victoria
Location: Islands off the coast of Africa, in the Indian Ocean
Area: 459,000 sq. km
Population: 95,654
Currency: Seychelles rupee
Languages: English, French and Seychellois Creole
Nationality: Seychellois

The Seychelles islands were first settled by the French in 1770. Seychelles islands were returned to the Britains under the treaty of Paris, in 1814, after the defeat of Napoleon. Its independence from Great Britain was achieved in 1976, when Seychelles became a republic. We can say that it is a young nation.

VICTORIA, SEYCHELLES.

1 Answer the following questions in your notebook.

a. Who were the first settlers of Seychelles islands?

b. Why can we say that Seychelles is a young nation?

c. What animal can be found only on Praslin Island?

2 Write the words from the box next to their meaning.

| law | parrot | archipelago |

a. A kind of bird: _____

b. A group of islands: _____

c. The system of rules of a country: _____

3 Read the article and underline the words related to fauna and flora.

Seychelles Flora & Fauna
Published in January 15

Seychelles is a living museum of natural history and a sanctuary for some of the rarest species of flora and fauna on Earth. It has conservation policies that have resulted in an enviable degree of protection for the environment and the varied ecosystems it supports.

Anywhere else on Earth you will find unique endemic specimens such as the fabulous Coco-de-mer, the largest seed in the world, the jellyfish tree, the Seychelles' paradise flycatcher and Seychelles' warbler.

Seychelles is also home to two Unesco World Heritage Sites and Aldabra, the world's largest raised coral reef, and Praslin's Vallée de Mai, that was once believed to be the original site of the Garden of Eden.

From the smallest frog to the heaviest land tortoise and the only flightless bird of the Indian Ocean, Seychelles protects a large endemic group species within surrounds of exceptional natural beauty.

Based on: <https://www.virtualmarket.itb-berlin.com/en/Flora-Fauna,p1220205>. Accessed on: Mar. 14, 2019.

LET'S LEARN MORE ABOUT AFRICA

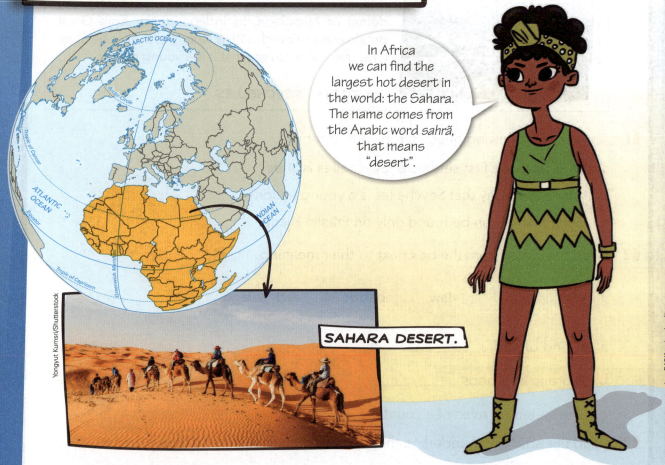

In Africa we can find the largest hot desert in the world: the Sahara. The name comes from the Arabic word *sahrã*, that means "desert".

SAHARA DESERT.

Did you know that Antarctica and the Arctic are also considered deserts? But they are both cold deserts, which makes the Sahara the third largest desert in the world.

It's about the size of the United States, covering 9.4 million square kilometers and is one of the harshest places on Earth.

The borders of the Sahara are: the Atlantic Ocean on the west, the Red Sea on the east, the Mediterranean Sea on the north and the Sahel Savannah on the south. It spreads through 11 different countries: Algeria, Chad, Egypt, Libya, Mali, Mauritania, Morocco, Niger, Western Sahara, Sudan and Tunisia.

Here are some interesting facts about the countries where we can see part of the Sahara Desert.

ALGERIA
The longest river in the country is the Chelif River, which runs from the Sahara and empties into the Mediterranean Sea.

CHAD
The Sahara covers most part of the north of the country and occupies roughly 1/3 of the country's total area.

EGYPT
The great pyramids were not built by slaves. They were paid laborers, and most of them built with great honor towards the pharaoh. Those who died while working, were buried in the tombs near the sacred pyramids.

LIBYA
Popular sports in Libya are soccer and chariot races. Camel racing is a common sport for desert nomads.

MALI
Rock paintings found in the region of Gao and Timbuktu suggest that the region of Mali was inhabited even around 50,000 BC.

MAURITANIA
The country is mostly a flat desert, with some hills in the center. The Sahara Desert covers 2/3 of the area.

MOROCCO
Morocco is only 13 kilometers from Europe, across the Strait of Gibraltar.

NIGER
The country of Niger is one of the hottest countries in the world and is famously nicknamed as "Frying Pan of the World".

WESTERN SAHARA
The general climate in Western Sahara is hot, dry with scarce rain. The cold offshore air currents produce fog and heavy dew.

SUDAN
There is a group of over 200 ancient pyramids, called the Meroë pyramids, after the Meroitic Kingdom that reigned over the area for over 900 years. They were built over 2,000 years ago.

TUNISIA
Tunisia has served as a popular location for some of Hollywood's biggest movies, such as *Star Wars*, *The English Patient* and *Indiana Jones' Raiders of the Lost Ark*.

Adapted from: <https://www.livescience.com/23140-sahara-desert.html>; <http://nationfacts.net/algeria-facts/>; <https://afrikanza.com/facts-about-chad/>; <https://www.swedishnomad.com/interesting-facts-about-egypt/>; <https://afrikanza.com/facts-about-libya/>; <https://factsking.com/countries/mali/>; <https://afrikanza.com/facts-about-mauritania/>; <https://afrikanza.com/facts-about-morocco/>; <https://factsking.com/countries/niger/>; <http://www.10-facts-about.com/Western-Sahara/id/957>; <http://nationfacts.net/sudan-facts/>. Accessed on: Mar. 14, 2019.

SOUTH AFRICA

CANGO CAVES

The Cango Caves are the oldest tourist attraction in South Africa and you can join an adventure tour to explore it.

On this tour, you'll go really deep into the cave. It's first part has over 200 steps that lead to the Grand Hall. Toward the end of the hall, you'll see a group of stalagmites.

Then you pass on to the Avenue to enter Lumbago Alley. It's 85 meters long and the height of the roof doesn't exceed 1,2 meters. And again you have some steps leading you to the chambers of King Solomon's Mines.

Be prepared, as you'll have to crawl to pass through the Tunnel of Love to get to the Ice Chamber. Next, you get to the Coffin and then the cave opens out again and you can see the walls decorated with many delicate helictites.

The way continues until you reach Devil's Kitchen to pass through the Devil's Chimney, which seems only a narrow crack in the wall. But that's where you have to squirm through to get to another, even smaller, opening.

You finally reach the Devil's Post Box, and you need to crawl to reach the only exit route. Which is 27 centimeters high. And then, you start it all over again, as the only way to actually leave the cave is by going back along the previous route to the cave entrance.

CANGO CAVES, SOUTH AFRICA.

Adapted from: <http://www.cango-caves.co.za/adventure.php>.
Accessed on: Mar. 14, 2019.

1 Number the sentences according to the tour's description above.

○ After seeing the stalagmites, you reach the Avenue.

○ The tour ends at the Devil's Post Box.

○ The way to the Ice Chamber passes through the Tunnel of Love.

○ The stairs after the Alley take you to the King Solomon's Mines.

○ The Grand Hall is after 200 steps.

○ After the tunnel, you get to Devil's Kitchen and Devil's Chimney.

○ Lumbago Alley is 85 meters long.

2 Answer the questions in your notebook.

a. What are the Cango Caves?

b. How high is the last part of the cave?

MAURITIUS

PORT LOUIS

People say the best way to know a country is by trying its food. And in Mauritius travelers (and locals!) can have some of the tastiest food ever! It is considered a great example of Creole cuisine and Mauritius is famous for its street food.

As people from different countries as China and France settled on the island, they brought with them the flavors of their homeland. When you walk on the streets of Port Louis you may find some familiar and some very peculiar dishes.

When you visit the island, make sure you try some typical Mauritian dishes as the octopus curry, the fish vindaye, the *boulet* (also known as *dim sum*), the *bol renverser* (or the upside-down bowl), the *dholl puri* and never skip a *gato piments*. These tiny balls of fried chilli are an iconic street food in Mauritius. The peas are mixed with spring onion, turmeric, and chilli and served on a warm baguette. If you want it a bit spicier, there's a drizzle of hot sauce.

Anytime of the day is a good time for a *gato piments*: breakfast, lunch and dinner! And, of course, always order some coconut water. Don't forget to ask for a coconut spoon so you can have the cream too.

Adapted from: <http://www.travelstart.co.za/blog/food-of-mauritius/>. Accessed on: Mar. 14, 2019.

MAURITIAN STREET FOOD.

1 Underline the correct option according to the text.

a. You can ask for a coconut **spoon/fork** to eat the coconut cream.

b. The *gato piments* is served on a **coconut/baguette**.

c. The most iconic street food in Mauritius is the **gato piments/octopus curry**.

d. Chinese and French people brought their **spoons/flavors** with them.

2 Complete the sentences with words from the box.

| food | hot | breakfast | streets |

a. You can have your *gato piments* with _____ sauce.

b. In Mauritius people can have the tastiest _____.

c. You find peculiar dishes on the _____ of Port Louis.

d. You can have *gato piments* for _____.

NIGERIA

IKOGOSI, EKITI STATE

IKOGOSI WARM SPRINGS, NIGERIA.

 The quiet and small town of Ikogosi, in the Ekiti State, is known national and now, internationally, because of the presence of warm and cold springs flowing side by side in the area.

 The spring is called Ikogosi Warm Spring and is a source of life for the local people and a source of revenue for the government.

 There are many tales about the flowing and the origin of the springs. One of them is that the spring were wives of the same husband, whom after much rivalry, were turned into water springs. The bad-tempered wife turned into the warm spring, and the calmer one became the cold spring. The surrounding hills as said to become the husband.

 Another story says that a powerful hunter discovered the warm spring, while hunting for animals in the bush. And a myth says that people got cured with the warm water, thus making people start to worship the water.

 But science explains it. The reason for the hot and cold springs is that the further water travels underground, the warmer it becomes. And the cold water comes from an adjoining hill. No matter what people believe in, the parallel flow of warm and cold springs is the only occurrence in the world.

Adapted from: <https://www.cometonigeria.com/wheretogo/ikogosi-warm-spring/>. Accessed on: Mar. 14, 2019.

1 Answer the questions in your notebook.

 a. What is Ikogosi famous for?

 b. Why is Ikogosi Warm Springs important for the government?

 c. Do people believe in tales and stories about the springs?

 d. Why some people worship the water?

 e. How science explains the hot water?

MOROCCO

RABAT

The capital city of Morocco is known as a city of music. Every year, there are free concerts with the biggest national and international celebrities. But the city pulses to the rhythm of world music all year long, so be sure you'll hear the sounds of Andalusia as well as the swing of jazz bands.

While exploring the city, visit the landmarks and monuments. While heading to the old town, known as the *medina*, check out the craftsmanship of the artisans. You'll find generations of artists working with fabric, leather, gold, silver and the celebrated Rabat carpets. These carpets are famous for their finesse and harmony, they're a masterpiece.

RABAT, MOROCCO.

Besides its city life, the beautiful beaches and the shopping, Rabat is also known for its green attitude. Nature has found a home in the heart of the city and can be seen in 570 acres of green spaces to enjoy nature and culture.

Visit the Kasbah of the Udayas to see the Andalusian garden, the Chellah necropolis, the green belt, the Ibn Sina park and the test gardens to see for yourself the perfect expression of nature. And just a few miles outside Rabat, the Bouknadel Exotic Gardens will also enchant you with its 11 acres and 600 different plant species from all over the world.

Adapted from: <https://www.visitmorocco.com/en/travel/rabat/culture/secrets-rbatis>. Accessed on: Mar. 14, 2019.

1 Complete the sentences with information from the text.

a. There are _____ concerts in the capital city of music.

b. The old _____ is called the *medina*.

c. The Rabat _____ are very famous for their harmony.

d. Rabat is known for its _____ attitude.

2 Match the two parts of the sentences.

a. In the Bouknadel Exotic Gardens

b. On the streets of Rabat, you can hear

c. You can go shopping and

○ to the beach in Rabat.

○ the sounds of Andalusia and the swing of jazz bands.

○ there are 600 different plant species.

EGYPT

FAYOUM

Fayoum, Egypt.

Now you don't need to travel long distances to go sand boarding in Egypt. Fayoum is located 90 kilometers from Cairo, it has a moderate weather all year round and it is one of Egypt's seven oases.

There you can find several attractions from different eras to varied activities as sand boarding, hiking and bird watching.

As it is an oasis, sand dunes are all over the place, so pick your spot and have some fun. Leave the adrenaline rush out of you while you're going down the dunes. The most famous sand boarding spot is Qoussour El-Arab.

But if you're looking for more adventure, then you should head to the Great Sand Sea, near Siwa. You'll find smooth and steep dunes that reach heights of 140 meters! But there are dunes of all shapes and sizes, and people can find the best dune for their surfing experience. Besides, you'll also have breathtaking views of the desert landscape as you glide.

A memorable experience that should be planned to happen between October and April as the weather can be really hot in the desert during summer time.

Adapted from: <http://www.egypt.travel/attractions/sand-boarding-in-the-great-sand-sea/>; <http://www.travelstart.com.eg/blog/fayoum-oasis-egypts-hidden-gem/>. Accessed on: Mar. 14, 2019.

1 Complete the information with one adjective, according to the text.

a. the weather in Fayoum: _____

b. the Qoussour El-Arab sand boarding spot: _____

c. the dunes in the Great Sand Sea: _____

d. the views in the Great Sand Sea: _____

e. the weather in the desert during summer: _____

2 Answer the questions.

a. Where is the Great Sand Sea?
_____

b. When is the best time to go sand surfing?
_____

c. Where is Fayoum located?
_____

KENYA

NAIVASHA

There's always a different way to see the animals and birds on a safari, so why not join a boat safari? A pleasant ride on Lake Naivasha can show you many beauties.

Lake Naivasha National Park is for bird lovers, but, even if you're not a huge fan of birds, you'll have a great time. If you're a photographer, this place will be your delight. You can get really close to the birds without scaring them.

People usually spend one hour sailing on the boat and are sad when the ride is over. And this is because they don't see only birds, but the lake is also known for its healthy population of hippos. It's very common to see them lazing in the swampy area of the lake and sometimes, it seems they are too close to the boat.

If you decide to stretch your legs a bit, you can go for a walk in the woods where the zebras, giraffes and waterbucks are snacking on grass. Just don't get to close not to disturb them.

And if you're still in doubt if it's worth it taking a boat tour, it's good to know that the boats have life jackets and are very clean and dry. Your camera equipment will be safe during the boat safari.

Adapted from: <http://www.tickingthebucketlist.com/2015/05/lake-naivasha-boat-safari.html>. Accessed on: Mar. 14, 2019.

LAKE NAIVASHA NATIONAL PARK, KENYA.

1 Circle the correct answer.

a. You can stretch your legs in the **boat/woods**.

b. There **are/aren't** many hippos in Lake Naivasha.

c. If you get to close to the birds you **scare/don't scare** them.

d. The boats are **dirty/clean**.

2 Find synonyms in the text for the following items.

a. a large antelope: _____

b. a nice ride: _____

c. the inhabitants of an area: _____

d. without any water: _____

TANZANIA

SERENGETI

Africa is known for its safaris, both by vehicle or by boat. But what about a balloon safari? It's a lifetime experience in northern Tanzania.

The hot air balloon rides leave from three different sites in the Serengeti. In Central Serengeti, see the Seronera River Valley where wildlife gathers throughout the year and there is permanent water. If you're planning to come around May and June you'll see the Great Migration.

The Western Serengeti includes the Grumeti River, where the theatrical crossings of the Great Migration happen in June and July.

SERENGETI NATIONAL PARK, TANZANIA.

In the South Serengeti plains, the wildebeests can be seen in December and in February, more than 8000 newborn every day on a three-week marathon. It can't be missed on your trip.

The plains of the Serengeti are suited to balloon flights and they are very convenient as you can have an aerial view of the action on the ground. It's a different view but you won't be missing anything that you could see if you are in a safari vehicle. You can probably startle some vultures by flying low over a flat-topped Acacia thorn tree. Maybe you can find the head of a giraffe as you over-fly the branches where they feed. And you'll be enchanted with the families of elephants in line, nose to tail, just as you see in the movies.

Adapted from: <https://www.africanmeccasafaris.com/travel-guide/tanzania/parks-reserves/serengeti/balloon-safari>. Accessed on: Mar. 14, 2019.

1 Complete the sentences with words from the box.

> giraffe   vehicle   action   weeks

a. In the hot air balloon you can have a view of the _____ on the ground.

b. You can see the head of a _____ when you fly over the branches.

c. Wildebeests are born every day, within two to three _____, during their anual migration in the Serengeti.

d. The aerial view is different from the view in a _____.

2 Answer the questions.

a. When is the Great Migration in Seronera River Valley?

b. When is the Great Migration in Grumeti River?

c. When can you see the newborn wildebeests?

d. How can you go on a safari in Tanzania?

SEYCHELLES

LA DIGUE

Beachcombing is a popular activity for people who like to spend their holidays at the seashore. It is to search for and collect objects along the seashore. The most common are shells, driftwood and sea glass, but many other treasures can be found along the seashore.

Many people that go to La Digue go beachcombing. The beautiful virgin beaches with fine white sand and the breathtaking coastline of Seychelles are also a plus in this different and relaxing activity.

But when going beachcombing, some recommendations should be followed. As you're on the beach, make sure you wear sunscreen and a hat. Even if you're used to staying in the sun, it's always good to play on the safe side.

LA DIGUE, SEYCHELLES.

Wear comfortable shoes if the area you're going to go beachcombing has too many rocks or slippery surfaces.

When taking something with you, make sure it is not someone's home! You'd be surprised at what crabs like to make their little houses out of.

Take a plastic bag with you to collect the garbage you may find. Beachcombing is not only about collecting beautiful things, you can also help to keep the beach clean and safe.

Adapted from: <http://www.iloveshelling.com/blog/category/world-shelling/indo-pacific-beach-combing/seychelle-islands-beach-comb-seashells/>; <http://www.seychellesapartment.com/seychelles/seychelles-islands-activities/>; <https://www.instructables.com/id/Guide-to-Beach-Combing/>. Accessed on: Mar. 14, 2019.

1 Write **T** (True) or **F** (False).

a. ◯ People that go beachcombing collect objects they find in the sand.

b. ◯ Beachcombing is an energetic activity.

c. ◯ You should wear sunscreen, a hat and comfortable shoes to go beachcombing.

d. ◯ People take plastic bags to collect the items they find.

2 Underline the correct option.

a. Crabs can make their houses in **shells/plastic bags**.

b. Beaches can have **dry/slippery** rocks and surfaces.

c. The coastline of Seychelles is **breathtaking/treasure**.

d. You can find **broken glass/sea glass** when beachcombing.

GLOSSARY

about: sobre
according to: de acordo com
achieve: alcançar
across: do outro lado
active: ativo/a
activity: atividade
actually: na realidade
adrenaline: adrenalina
adventure: aventura
after: após
again: novamente
ago: atrás (no passado)
air: ar
almost: quase
always: sempre
amazing: incrível
ancient: antigo
another: outro/a
answer: responder; resposta
anytime: a qualquer hora
anywhere: em qualquer lugar
approach: aproximar
archipelago: arquipélago
ark: arca
around: em torno de
article: artigo
artisan: artesão
artist: artista
ask: perguntar
attitude: atitude
attraction: atração
authentic: autêntico/a
away: daqui/de distância

bad: ruim
bad-tempered: mal--humorado/a
bag: sacola
baguette: baguete
balloon: balão
band: banda
be in a hurry: estar com pressa
beach: praia
beachcombing: procurar coisas na praia
beautiful: bonito/a
beauty: beleza
became: tornar
because: porque
bed: cama
beginning: início

believe: acreditar
belt: cinto
besides: além de
between: entre
birdwatching: observação de pássaros
bit: pedaço
blank: espaço em branco
block: quadra
boat: barco
body: corpo
border: fronteira
boring: chato/a; entediante
both: ambos
botton: parte de baixo
bowl: tigela
box: caixa
branch: galho
breakfast: café da manhã
breathtaking: deslumbrante
British: britânico/a
buck: dólar
buffalo: búfalo
bury: enterrar
bush: matagal
but: mas

camel: camelo
camera: câmera
capital: capital
cargo: carregamento
carpet: tapete
castle: castelo
cave: caverna
celebrity: celebridade
centimeter: centímetro
century: século
chamber: câmara
championship: campeonato
chariot: carruagem
cheetah: guepardo
chilli: pimenta
chimney: chaminé
choose: escolher
city: cidade
claim: alegar
clean: limpo/a
climate: clima
climb: escalar
climbing: alpinismo
coast: costa
coconut: coco
coffin: caixão
cold: frio; resfriado
collect: colecionar
colored: de cor; colorido/a
come from: vir de

comfortable: confortável
common: comum
complex: complexo
comprise: abranger
concert: concerto
conservation: conservação
consider: considerar
construction: construção
continent: continente
continue: continuar
convenient: conveniente
corpse: cadáver
correct: correto/a
cost: custar
cough: tosse
could: poderia
country: país
cover: cobrir
crab: caranguejo
crack: rachadura
crawl: rastejar; arrastar-se
cream: creme
crossing: travessia
cuisine: cozinha
culture: cultura
cure: curar
curiosity: curiosidade
currency: moeda
current: corrente

dark: escuro/a
deal: lidar
decorate: decorar
deep: fundo/a
defeat: derrota
definitely: com certeza
degree: grau
delicate: delicado/a
delight: prazer
desert: deserto
devil: demônio
dew: orvalho
dialog: diálogo
die: morrer
different: diferente
dinner: jantar
directions: direção
discover: descobrir
dish: prato
distance: distância
disturb: perturbar
dominant: dominante
doubt: dúvida
driftwood: madeira levada pela correnteza
drink: beber
driver: motorista

drizzle: chuvisco
dry: seco
dune: duna
during: durante

Earth: Terra
east: leste
eastern: do leste; oriental
easy: fácil
ecosystem: ecossistema
elephant: elefante
empty: vazio; esvaziar
enchant: encantar
enchanted: encantado/a
end: fim; acabar
endangered: ameaçado/a de extinção
endemic: endêmico/a
enjoy: desfrutar de; curtir
enter: entrar
enthusiastic: entusiasmado/a
entrance: entrada
enviable: invejável
environment: meio ambiente
equipment: equipamento
ethnic: étnico/a
even: até
ever: alguma vez
every: todo/a
everyone: todos/as
exceed: exceder
exceptional: excepcional
excited: animado/a
exciting: emocionante
excuse me: desculpe-me
exist: existir
exit: saída
exotic: exótico/a
expanse: extensão
experienced: experiente
expert: especialista
explain: explicar
explore: explorer
explosion: explosão
expression: expressão

fabric: tecido
fabulous: fabuloso/a
fact: fato
false: falso/a
famous: famoso/a
famously: famosamente

30

fantastic: fantástico/a
feed: alimentar
feel: sentir
few: alguns
fill in: preencher
finally: finalmente
finals: final
find: encontrar
fine: fino/a
finesse: requinte
first-time: primeira vez
fish: peixe
flat: plano
flight: voo
flightless: não voador/a
floor: chão
flow: fluxo
fly: voar
fog: neblina
follow: seguir
food: comida
football: futebol
free: grátis
fried: frito/a
friend: amigo/a
further: mais; em grau mais elevado

garbage: lixo
garden: jardim
garlic: alho
gather: reunir-se
generation: geração
get on: subir (em algo)
get: chegar
giraffe: girafa
give: dar
go: ir
gold: de ouro; ouro
good luck: boa sorte
good: bom
government: governo
grass: grama
great: ótimo/a
ground: chão
group: grupo

hall: entrada
hand: mão
harmony: harmonia
harsh: áspero/a; rigoroso/a
hat: chapéu
have: ter
healthy: saudável
hear: ouvir
heavy: pesado/a; intenso/a
height: altura
help: ajudar

here: aqui
heritage: patrimônio
high: alto
hiking: caminhada
hill: colina
hippo: hipopótamo
history: história
homeland: terra natal
honor: honra
horn: chifre
hot: quente
how: como
how much: quanto
hunter: caçador/a
hunting: caçar
husband: marido

ice: gelo
iconic: icônico/a
in fact: na realidade
incorrect: incorreto/a
independence: independência
inhabit: habitar
inside: no interior; dentro
instruction: instrução
interesting: interessante
internationally: internacionalmente
island: ilha

join: juntar
just: apenas

keep: manter
kilometer: quilômetro
king: rei
kitchen: cozinha
know: conhecer; saber

laborer: operário/a
lake: lago
landmark: marco
landscape: paisagem
language: idioma
last: último
law: lei
lead: conduzir
league: liga
learn: aprender
leather: couro
leave: partir
left: esquerdo/a

leg: perna
life jacket: colete salva-vidas
lifetime: existência
line: fila
linen: linho
lion: leão
liquid: líquido
living: vivo
locate: estar localizado/a
location: localização
long: longo/a
look for: procurar
lost: perdido/a
lots (of): muitos/as
low: baixo
lucky: com sorte
lunch: almoço

ma'am: senhora
main: principal
majority: maioria
make: fazer
many: muitos/as
marathon: maratona
masterpiece: obra-prima
match: combinar
may: poder
mean: significar
meaning: significado
medal: medalha
memorable: memorável
merchant: comerciante
meter: metro
million: milhão
mint: menta
mix: misturar
moderate: moderado/a
monastery: monastério
monument: monumento
more: mais
more than: mais que
mostly: principalmente
mountain: montanha
mouth: boca
movie: filme
mummy: múmia
music: música
myth: mito

narrow: estreito/a
nationality: nacionalidade
native: nativo/a
nature: natureza
near: perto
nearby: perto; próximo/a
neck: pescoço
necropolis: necrópole
need: precisar

never: nunca
newborn: recém-nascido/a
next: próximo/a
nickname: apelido; apelidar
no matter: não importa
nomad: nômade
none: nenhum/nenhuma
northeast: nordeste
northern: do norte
nose: nariz

occupy: ocupar
occurrence: ocorrência
ocean: oceano
octopus: polvo
of course: é claro
official: oficial
offload: livrar-se
offshore: oceânico
olympic: olímpico
once: uma vez
onion: cebola
only: somente
open: abrir; aberto/a
opening: abertura
order: ordem; pedir
origin: origem
other: outro
outside: fora de
own: próprio

painting: pintura
parallel: paralelo
parrot: papagaio
participate: participar
pass: passar
patient: paciente
pay: pagar
pea: ervilha
perfect: perfeito/a
period: período
permanent: permanente
person: pessoa
pharaoh: faraó
photographer: fotógrafo/a
place: lugar
plastic: plástico/a
pleasant: agradável
poach: caça predatória
policy: política
populate: habitar
population: população
populous: populoso/a
pound: libra
powerful: poderoso/a
precious: precioso/a
prepare: preparar
presence: presença
process: processo

31

protect: proteger
protection: proteção
pulse: pulso; pulsar
put: colocar
pyramid: pirâmide

quiet: calmo/a

race: corrida
racism: racismo
ranger: guarda florestal
rare: raro/a
reach: alcançar
read: ler
ready: pronto/a
really: de verdade
reason: razão
recipe: receita
recommendation: recomendação
reef: recife
region: região
reign: reinar; reinado
relate: relacionar
related: relacionado/a
relaxing: relaxante
remove: remover
republic: república
rest: descansar
result: resultado
revenue: receita
rhino: rinoceronte
rhythm: ritmo
ride: andar de (barco, balão)
right: direita
rivalry: rivalidade
rock: pedra
roof: teto
roughly: aproximadamente
route: rota
rule: regra
run: correr
runner: corredor/a

sacred: sagrado/a
safe: seguro/a
salesperson: vendedor/a
sanctuary: reserva; santuário
sand: areia
sauce: molho
scarce: escasso/a
scaring: assustar
scenario: cenário
science: ciência
seaglass: vidro; cristal marinho

search: procurar
seashore: litoral; costa
see: ver
seed: semente
sentence: frase
separation: separação
serve: servir
settle: estabelecer-se
several: vários/as
shape: forma
shell: concha
shoe: sapato
sick: doente
sickness: doença
side: lado
side by side: lado a lado
silver: prata
site: sítio
situation: situação
size: tamanho
skin: pele
skip: pular
slave: escravizado/a
sleep: dormir
slippers: pantufas
slippery: escorregadio/a
small: pequeno/a
smooth: macio/a
snorkeling: mergulho usando tubo de respiração
soccer: futebol
sore throat: dor de garganta
sound: som
source: fonte
south: sul
speak: falar
specially: especialmente
species: espécies
specimen: espécime
spend: gastar
spice: condimento
spoon: colher
sport: esporte
spot: identificar
spread: estender
spring: primavera
square: quadrado/a
squirm: contorcer-se
stalagmite: estalagmite
start: começar
startle: assustar
step: degrau
still: ainda
stop: parar
story: história
strait: estreito/a
stranded: abandonado/a
street: rua
stretch: esticar
strip: listra; faixa
such as: por exemplo
suggest: sugerir
summer: verão
summit: cume

sunscreen: protetor solar
support: apoio
sure: certamente
surfaces: superfícies
surfing: surfar
surround: cercar
surrounding: dos arredores
swampy: pantanoso/a
swim: nadar
swing: balançar-se
system: sistema

tail: rabo
tale: conto
tasty: saboroso/a
tea: chá
team: time
the most: o/a mais
theatrical: teatral
then: em seguida
there is/are: há
there: lá
these: esses
thing: coisa
think: pensar
third: terceiro
thorn: espinho
those: aqueles
throat: garganta
through: através de
throughout: por toda a parte
times: vezes
tiny: minúsculo/a
tomb: tumba
tomorrow: amanhã
too fast: muito rápido/a
top: topo
tour: passeio
tourist: turista
towards: em direção a
town: cidade
travel: viajar
travel agent: agente de viagem
treasure: tesouro
treaty: acordo; tratado
tree: árvore
tribe: tribo
trip: viagem
true: verdadeiro/a
try: experimentar; tentar
turmeric: cúrcuma
turn: virar
turned into: transformar alguém; algo
typical: típico

under: sob; embaixo

underground: subterrâneo
underline: sublinhar
unique: único/a
until: até
upside down: de cabeça para baixo

vacation: férias
varied: variado/a
vehicle: veículo
very: muito/a
view: vista
virgin: virgem
visit: visitar
volcanic: vulcânico/a
vulture: abutre

wait: esperar
walk: caminhar
wall: parede; muro
want: querer
warm: quente
watch: assistir
water: água
way: caminho
wear: usar; vestir
weather: clima
welcome: bem-vindo/a
west: oeste
western: ocidental
what: o que
when: quando
where: onde
which: qual
while: enquanto
white: branco/a
whom: quem
why: por que
wife: esposa
wildebeest: gnu
wildlife: fauna
win: vencer
wish: querer que; desejar; desejo
with: com
within: dentro de
wood: bosque
world: mundo
worship: venerar
worth: valer algo
write: escrever

year: ano
young: jovem